ALCATRAZ
BELIEVE IT OR NOT

T. C. BAKKER

Timber

ILLUSTRATED BY
CHARLES HOUSE

GOLDEN GATE NATIONAL PARKS CONSERVANCY

SAN FRANCISCO, CALIFORNIA

Published in the United States by
Golden Gate National Parks Conservancy
Building 201 Fort Mason
San Francisco, California 94123
www.parksconservancy.org

ISBN 978-1-932519-36-5
Library of Congress Control Number: 2015936439

Photos used in this book come from a variety of sources, some of which may
require permission to reproduce. For more information, contact the source cited.
Golden Gate National Parks Conservancy Collection:
pp. 51, 70 (Nate Fowle), 96, 97 (Nate Fowle)
Golden Gate National Recreation Area/Park Archives and Records Center:
pp. 15; 17 (P89-052.235n); 25 (GOGA 2316); 31 (Fischetti Collection, GOGA 18352.013); 41
(Interp. photos, Box 1); 71–72 (Wallar Collection, GOGA 19200.340 & GOGA 19200.152);
73 (Fischetti Collection, GOGA 18352); 76; 85 (P85-060.4); 93; 95, federal penitentiary
era, occupation era (GOGA 18488.001); 102; 104, dummy head, (P85.060.6) & back of
cell; 105 (Bowden Collection)
National Archives and Records Administration: pp. 32–35, 42, 47, 62, 74, 81
Wikimedia Commons: p. 95, NPS era (Tewy)

Art Direction: Robert Lieber, Vivian Young
Design, Illustrations: Charles House
Editor: Susan Tasaki
Production Coordinator: Sarah Lau Levitt

Developed and Designed in the United States
Printed in Hong Kong

PARKS FOR ALL FOREVER™

CONTENTS

PROTEST SITE ALCATRAZ

NATIONAL PARK ALCATRAZ

To Chelsea Fern and Nate

ALCATRAZ ISLAND

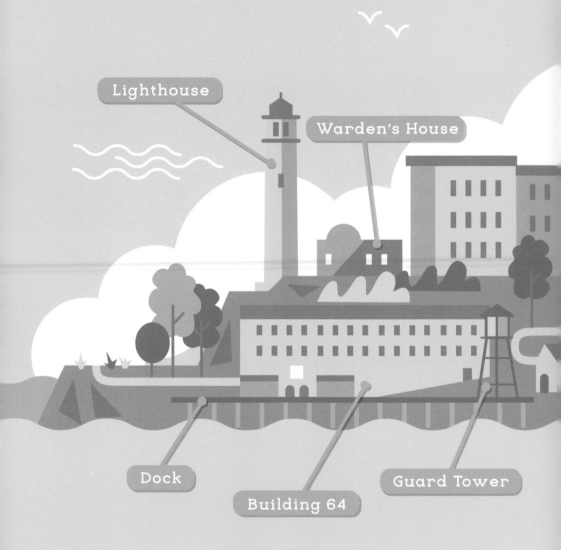

Lighthouse

Warden's House

Dock

Building 64

Guard Tower

Water Tower

Cellhouse

Model Industries Building

Powerhouse

Sally Port

Quartermaster

ALCATRAZ THROUGH TIME

Believe it or not, for most of its life, no one cared about Alcatraz Island. Other than to (maybe) gather bird eggs, native people had no reason to paddle to it in their reed boats. It held no dreamers or schemers, no one with stories to tell or stories to hide. That would come later.

To begin with, Alcatraz was a small hill in a large valley. Then, after the last ice age, sea levels rose and water gradually covered the valley, creating San Francisco Bay. Some of the hilltops—including Alcatraz—became islands.

When gold was discovered in 1848 at Sutter's Mill, about 130 miles northeast of the bay, the race for wealth was on. During the California Gold Rush (1848–1855), people came west on ships, on trains, and on foot, eager to get rich. San Francisco quickly grew into a big Wild West city, full of the needy and greedy, the heroic and hopeful. Suddenly, Alcatraz Island, right smack in line with the Golden Gate, looked good to someone: the United States Army. The island was in a perfect place to protect San Francisco Bay, which almost overnight had become the world's most valuable port.

Beginning in 1853, the army blasted cliffs, mounted cannons, and stationed soldiers. But no one attacked, and after a while, Alcatraz became a handy place to keep military prisoners. Miserable, pickax-swinging men broke rock from dawn 'til dusk, watched over by armed military guards. With people came stories: prisoners' stories, soldiers' stories, even children's stories. Officers and their families lived on the island, too, and their children swapped tales, told secrets, and explored their island home's nooks and crannies.

PROPERTY
U.S. ARMY

In 1933, to fight organized (and disorganized) crime, the federal Bureau of Prisons took over Alcatraz; the following year, it opened the country's first "super-max" prison there. Behind the concrete building's solid walls, the bureau hid America's most dangerous inmates: murderers; con men, gangsters, and, most importantly, plotters and planners. Some of the "worst of the worst" were also the "best of the best" at escaping. When inmates entered the prison, they had to pass through five locked doors. Inside, they exchanged their stories in whispers (at first, there was a no-talking-in-the-cellhouse rule, so they had to be sneaky). Just down the hill, where the guards' families lived, children shouted and played, and shared their own stories with friends.

The prison closed in 1963 and, for a while, all was quiet. Then, in 1969, young American Indian protesters jumped off a boat and swam to the island. They knew that if they took over Alcatraz, their story would become worldwide news, which is just what they wanted. In 1971, the last of the occupiers were taken off the island by government agents, and it was once again a quiet place.

A year later, Alcatraz became part of the new Golden Gate National Recreation Area, protected by the National Park Service and its rangers. No one imagined that anyone would want to see the old prison, but today, more than a million people come from all over the world to visit it every year. They explore the prison building, walk through the restored gardens, take in the views. But mostly, they come to hear the stories. In more than 160 years, a lot of strange and unusual things can happen, and a lot did.

Many of the island's stories have been gathered in this book, and they're all true . . . believe it or not!

FORT
ALCATRAZ

SIX WAYS FORT ALCATRAZ WAS LIKE
A CASTLE OF YORE

It's funny to think that Alcatraz started its life as a place to keep people out, not a place to keep people in. Alcatraz was a lot like the old and famous castles in Europe.

① CLIFFS

Many castles are built on cliffs—cliffs are hard to climb. Alcatraz originally was a small, rounded island in the bay. The first thing the army did was to blast cliffs all the way around the island, making it difficult for attackers to climb to the top.

② DRAWBRIDGE AND MOAT

Many castles have drawbridges and moats. On Alcatraz, enemy ships could only land at the dock. Then, attackers would have had to charge across the drawbridge and moat and through the sally port. A drawbridge works two ways. Not only is it a bridge, but when it's pulled up, it becomes a sturdy shield that's hard to smash open with a battering ram.

A moat can work two ways, too. Some moats are filled with water. Since long ago, many people couldn't swim, a moat was a nearly impassable barrier. But there are also "dry moats," like those at Alcatraz. These are deep holes that an enemy has to climb into (and out of) to get to a building. Once the enemy was below ground level in a dry moat, it was easy to shoot them or throw things on them—and hard for them to get out, to retreat, or to run away.

③ WEAPON SLITS

Castles had openings called "arrow slits," which made it easy for men to hide while firing on the enemy. On Alcatraz, the openings were called "rifle slits," and they gave soldiers the same protection.

YE OLDE CASTLE

④ SALLY PORT

Many castles had sally ports, or secured entryways. If the men broke down the drawbridge and got past the doors, they were stuck inside a narrow room with another set of doors on the far side, where deadly arrows could be rained down upon them.

At Alcatraz, once the enemy got past the drawbridge, moat, and rifle slits by the water, they then had to face them all over again at the citadel on the top of the island, which also had those things.

The big concrete prison building has some of these same features. Prisons often have a series of sally ports, or gates, between one area and another. That way, prisoners can be controlled as they're being moved around. Prisons also have rifle slits, which are called gun ports.

⑤ BRICK WALLS

Most people think of castles as being made of stone, but as far back as the 1400s, even very large castles were built with brick. Malbork Castle in Poland is the largest brick building in Europe today.

The Alcatraz citadel was made of brick, though many retaining walls were made from large blocks of sandstone quarried on nearby Angel Island

⑥ PARAPETS AND CATWALKS

Running around the edge of a castle's outside walls was something called a parapet. Soldiers on the parapet could look down on the enemy and were in a great position to fire arrows or lob buckets of hot oil down on them.

The prison building on Alcatraz had catwalks that were like a castle's parapets. Catwalks lined the edges of the building, both inside and outside, as well as the walls around the recreation yard. From the catwalks, guards could look down on the inmates and keep weapons trained on them.

FORT ALCATRAZ

A PRISONER OF WAR, FOREVER

In 1873, a teenager named Barncho was about to change the lives of his people, the Modoc.

The Modoc lived in Northern California, in a harsh land covered with black lava rocks as sharp as knives. Below the ground was a labyrinth of caves that the Modoc knew well.

In April of that year, Barncho's people were in the midst of a war. Captain Jack, their leader, was to meet with leaders from the American military under the white flag of peace, but the rest of his tribe wanted blood. Years earlier, Americans flying the flag of peace had tricked the Modoc. Though they said they would come unarmed, they had weapons and fired upon helpless men, women, and children, slaughtering many. The brokenhearted Modoc never forgot, and most never forgave.

Their second meeting was also to be without weapons, but this time, the Modoc would do the tricking. The leaders met in a tent in the middle of a field. At a signal, Barncho and another young warrior named Slolux did what they had been told to do: jumped out of their hiding places and gave rifles to the Indian leaders. The Modoc leaders killed several officers and ran off. The American military came back with a vengeance . . . and hundreds of soldiers.

The Modoc War was misery for the American soldiers. The sharp lava shredded their shoes and clothes and skin. There was no place to hide. The weather could be fiery hot in the day and icy cold at night. The Modoc knew how to jump out of the caves unseen, attack, and disappear. They seemed magical, invincible.

But they weren't. Eventually, the outnumbered Modoc lost the war, and Barncho, Slolux, and four Modoc leaders went to trial. The leaders were hanged, and in 1873, Barncho and Slolux were sent to Alcatraz.

How strange that must have been for Barncho, a young man who had never been away from his homeland or known anyone outside of his small tribe.

He was taken on a train to a crowded city and put on a boat bound for the lonely prison island of Alcatraz.

One of the American soldiers who took part in the Modoc war was a young man named John Long. It's unlikely that he knew Barncho, but he and Barncho had surely fought against one another. John Long, like most soldiers, detested that war, and decided that he would desert his post. He stole several hundred dollars from fellow soldiers and ran away to San Francisco, where, unluckily for him, he was caught. He was then sent to Alcatraz Island to await trial.

John Long couldn't face the shame and humiliation of a court martial and prison. In early 1875, he hanged himself in his cell. Because he never went to trial, he was buried on nearby Angel Island with full military honors.

Four months later, his former adversary, Barncho, joined him there. Barncho had died of tuberculosis, and, like John Long, was buried on Angel Island. For seventy years, they were quiet and peaceful neighbors. In 1947, the military moved all the bodies to a new cemetery in San Bruno, many miles away.

Though Barncho's grave is in the midst of Golden Gate National Cemetery, it is a lonely grave indeed. His headstone is inscribed in a language he did not understand. It has a Christian cross, a symbol of a religion he did not believe in. And once again, he is surrounded by his enemies.

Is Barncho a prisoner of war, forever?

ALCATRAZ'S *1,000-Year-Old* PERUVIAN PRINCESS

She may not have been a princess, but she was surely someone important.

How in the world did she—or, at least, her mummified head—end up on Alcatraz Island?

In 1873, the German sailing ship *Matthais Mayer* left England on its way to San Francisco. It had to sail all the way down and around the southern tip of South America and then north again to California: a long trip. It stopped in Peru to drop off a load of coal and pick up a load of sugar. But something went wrong, and the sugar deal didn't go through. The captain had to find something else to load into the ship's cargo hold.

Old wooden sailing ships had heavy sails and masts, and needed weight (ballast) to keep them from tipping over.

The captain bought bags of sand for ballast, but little did he know that the sand contained arm bones, skulls, and mummified legs!

Sailors in those days were mighty superstitious. If they had known they would be traveling over the waves with mummies, they would never have left port.

Once the ship got to San Francisco, the sailors innocently unloaded the ballast, and sand, bones, and skulls poured out onto the wharf. Crowds gathered. Some cried out "Murderers!"

Eventually, the bystanders were convinced that these were very old bones, not recent murder victims.

Where did the bones and mummies come from? How did they get into the sand?

A year earlier, when a railroad cut was being built to Ancon, Peru, an ancient burial ground was uncovered. In the sand were treasures, a bit like those found in the Egyptian pyramids. Mummies were buried with jewelry, cloth, pottery, even corn on the cob.

Within weeks, people came from all over the world to shovel up the treasures. If you thought an item was valuable or interesting, you kept it and took it home.

A year later, German scientists rushed to dig up the remaining items so they could preserve and study them. They took the artifacts back to a museum in Germany, where they still are today. They learned that the burials were 500 to 4,000 years old.

When the grisly artifacts landed on the San Francisco dock, onlookers began collecting them. Some picked up skulls and walked away with them.

One soldier retrieved a particularly gruesome relic to take to the army doctor on Alcatraz for his "collection." It was a woman's mummified head, with long, curly hair!

Did the Peruvian woman's head look out mournfully across the bay from the doctor's office on the windswept island of Alcatraz? Was she forever separated from the rest of her body in the museum in Germany, 6,000 miles away, so far from her home?

And where is her head now?

ALCATRAZ FOUGHT AN

It was July 4, 1876, and everyone was looking forward to celebrating the 100th birthday of the United States.

    In San Francisco, friends and families gathered, packed picnics, and headed to the hills overlooking the bay. The army was going to put on a special "fireworks" display.

    Floating in the bay was an old schooner full of explosives. At a signal, it was to be blown up by cannons firing from both Fort Alcatraz and Fort Point, which sat across the water near the city.

    For years, the people of San Francisco had rested easy, knowing they were protected by the massive firepower at both forts. The city had never been attacked, so the cannons had never been used against an enemy. But the citizens knew that if anyone did attack, they would surely be defeated.

    Now the cannons and soldiers would finally be tested in a "mock battle."

    The time and the signal came, and the cannons were set off. Blasts of smoke rose above Fort Point and Alcatraz and drifted across the bay. Cannonballs splashed in the water . . . nowhere near the schooner! Again and again, the cannons fired. Again and again, they missed. Alcatraz's cannon were especially far off. The

IMAGINARY ENEMY
(AND LOST!)

crowds began to laugh. Good thing this was a mock battle—the "enemy ship" hadn't even moved.

The military men were embarrassed.

Nothing they did worked. They could not get close to hitting that schooner.

Massive clouds of cannon smoke hovered over the bay. The citizens didn't know whether to be horrified or amused. These were the forts that had been protecting them?

At last, a young officer was sent out in a boat. He set a charge on the schooner, lit a fuse, and hurried away. Finally, the ship exploded. By then, many of the people watching had already gone home.

The mock battle was over, but it was the subject of many jokes and scathing newspaper articles for days.

How lucky that for all those years, these fortifications never came under attack!

NINETEEN HOPI FATHERS, NINETEEN SUPERHEROES

By the 1890s, the Indian Wars were mostly over, and the Indians had lost. Most had been uprooted from their homes and moved to reservations, which were barren lands nobody else wanted. Some of the tribes were not allowed to hunt or farm, and had to rely on the government to feed them.

The government believed it was right to force the Indians to become like white people. It wanted them to forget their religion, their dances, their ceremonies, even their languages.

They were forced to cut their hair and throw away their native clothes. They were to become "Americanized."

The government thought that one easy way to make this happen was to remove children—some as young as five—from their families and send them to boarding schools far away. They were not allowed to see their parents for years at a time.

These schools were overcrowded. Sometimes, diseases killed the children. Sometimes, the children went hungry. Sometimes, the children were beaten if they spoke their native language or prayed in their own way. If they did have a chance to visit their families, they were no longer able to talk to them because they had forgotten their native language. This was exactly what the government wanted to happen.

One day in 1894, American soldiers came to the Hopi Reservation to pick up their children and take them to boarding school. But the children had vanished. Their fathers had hidden them. The Hopi fathers had had enough. Even if it meant they might starve, they would not let their children be taken away.

On November 25th, 1894, the government arrested nineteen Hopi men and sentenced them to hard labor on Alcatraz Island. They were to remain there until "they fully realize the error of their evil ways."

The men toiled on the Rock for eight months. Occasionally, they were taken to San Francisco, where they visited schools and parks and attended concerts. Many of the city's citizens probably gawked at the men.

Finally, they were released and returned to their families.

What happened to their children? Did they return to their families? Were they kept in hiding? Or did the government finally find them and send them away to the boarding schools their fathers had tried so hard to keep them out of?

For now, history is silent. Neither historians nor Hopi descendants have—or will share—the answer to this question.

It remains a mystery.

The nineteen Hopi fathers.

THE DEVIL ON DEVIL'S ISLAND

During the military years, Alcatraz was known as "Uncle Sam's Devil's Island."

Was there a devil on Devil's Island? Perhaps.

We like to think of lighthouse keepers as being diligent, hardworking, and kind. But one of the Alcatraz lighthouse keepers, Benjamin Leeds, was said to be quite devilish. In fact, he was so hard on his assistants that no one would work for him. In five years, he went through twenty-five assistant lighthouse keepers—one every two or three months!

Why would no one work for him? Surely, many men must have wanted the job. The lighthouse keeper must have been ghastly indeed.

Then, the unthinkable happened. James T. Moran was the new assistant. He had a wife and son, was well liked, and had many friends from his earlier army years. On his third day of work, Moran went missing. What ghoulish thing had happened? He was discovered in a small building near the lighthouse. He had sliced his own throat with a serrated knife. His wife and friends were shocked. What horrible thing could possibly have happened with the lighthouse keeper in only three days? We'll never know.

Lighthouse keeper Benjamin Leeds in front of the first Alcatraz lighthouse; the citadel is in the background.

MILITARY PRISON
ALCATRAZ

BUMBLING ESCAPES, BRAINY ESCAPES

Some of the more creative escapes from Alcatraz happened during the military prison years. Perhaps because the island wasn't a high-security prison at that time, guards were a bit less guarded.

One of these escapes involved a common kitchen item.

Can you imagine trying to feed all of the men on Alcatraz Island? The cooks, who were also prisoners, baked hundreds of loaves of bread and cooked stews in enormous tubs.

In fact, the wooden trough they used to mix bread dough was so large that four men could fit into it. And that gave them an idea ... not a good idea, but an idea.

They thought they could escape from the island by using the bread trough as a boat.

Early one evening, the four prisoners broke out of their cells, fled to the water's edge, and boarded their "boat."

The moment they got into it, it sank, dumping them into the cold water. Found hiding in an abandoned building the next morning, they were clapped in irons and returned to the prison. So much for "Rub a dub dub, *four* men in a tub!"

Another creative escape involved a counterfeiter.

Counterfeiters are people who break the law by printing things that look real—money, for example. But this counterfeiter didn't want money; he wanted to get out of prison. He realized he could actually print his own one-way ticket off Alcatraz, and help out three of his prisoner friends at the same time.

These four prisoners worked together in a printing shop, printing things the army needed, such as posters and forms and labels. This gave the counterfeiter an idea . . . a good idea. He knew that the warden received "release papers." These were papers sent by the War Department in Washington, D.C., that told the warden that a prisoner had completed his prison time and was to be released.

The counterfeiter simply printed up releases for himself and his three friends. It worked! They were congratulated, given a set of clothes and some money, and even taken to San Francisco in an army boat.

His three friends were handed their freedom on a silver platter, but they couldn't hold onto it. They weren't as crafty as the counterfeiter. They only went as far as nearby restaurants and bars and spent their money having fun, with no thought to the future. The army soon discovered the ruse, nabbed the three prisoners, and brought them back.

But the counterfeiter spent his money on a real one-way ticket out of town. He was never seen again.

A third creative escape used a simple box.

A prisoner named Adams was working outside as a gardener when he noticed a large empty box in a shed. It was addressed to a hospital across the bay. He stowed himself in the box, then had a fellow prisoner nail on the lid and haul the heavy box to the dock. It was loaded onto the steamer *McDowell*.

Adams was lucky in three ways: first, finding the box; second, that the box was marked "Handle with Care!"; and third, that when it arrived at the hospital, it wasn't opened right away, but instead, was stored in a shed.

The next morning, one empty box was found in the hospital shed, and one prisoner was missing from Alcatraz. It was pretty easy for everyone to put one and one together. Adams was never found.

Forget blasting your way out of prison with a machine gun, or jumping into the bay.

Brainy escapes are the most successful of all!

Tom the Mule's
FINAL STEP

Can animals have thoughts and feelings like people? Alcatraz soldiers and officers believed so, when, in 1920, they had a full military funeral for Mike the Mule.

Before Alcatraz had trucks, it had mule carts, and Alcatraz was built by the pulling power of Tom and Mike, two mules who toiled side by side for fifteen years.

Mike was always harnessed on the "haw" side (the left) and his best buddy Tom was always to the right ("gee" side). Even when they grazed high on the island, they grazed side by side, Tom on the gee and Mike on the haw.

One day in February 1920, Mike got "mule flu" and died. Tom ran his nose over his best friend, and the stable sergeant swore he saw tears in Tom's eyes.

The men saw Mike as a fellow soldier and gave him a proper funeral. They also decided that Tom could now retire and enjoy the rest of his days grazing lazily. The problem was, he looked miserable. The doughboys (a nickname for soldiers at that time) tried their best to raise his spirits, but nothing seemed to work.

On February 16, 1920, Tom was in his pasture near the top of the island, gazing sadly at ships in the bay far below. He walked toward the fifty-foot cliff, paused for just a moment, then deliberately stepped off.

The doughboys raced to him, but he was dead.

Colonel Johnson, officer of the prison barracks, told newspaper reporters that Tom knew the cliff was there—it was a clear case of suicide.

Is it possible? Did a mule commit suicide on Alcatraz Island?

DOUBLE DEATH
IN BUILDING 64

MURDER, MADNESS, OR MISTAKE?

At 10:30 one morning in 1920, a soldier, Private Davis, was sitting in his barracks room in Alcatraz's Building 64, looking out the window.

Suddenly, he was shocked to see a man plunge headfirst past his window, followed by a horrifying crash on the hard metal grating, thirty feet below.

And so began a strange and tragic mystery.

Soldiers ran to the man. Thomas Mullaly, clerk of the Third Company, lay dying on the grating where he landed.

Soon after, the men heard cries from Thomas's roommate, Quartermaster Sergeant Roy Ford, who ran down the stairs from above, saying that Thomas had fallen out of the window. When he got to his bunkmate's side and saw the condition he was in, he cried out, "My God! What shall I do?" and ran off.

The post doctor showed up and declared Thomas Mullaly dead. Now there was a search for Roy Ford. Everyone thought that Thomas had simply fallen out of the window. So why had Roy run away? Where did he go?

The men searched high and low. Roy wasn't in his room or in any other obvious place on the island. At last, someone noticed a movement behind the open door of a storeroom. They headed toward it, but the door slammed shut.

And then there was a gunshot blast! Roy Ford had killed himself.

What had happened?

The investigators asked some questions. These are the six things they found out:

1 Everyone said the men were the best of friends.

2 Neither of the men was in any kind of trouble.

3 No one heard them arguing before Thomas fell. In fact, they had been talking politely just a few minutes before they went up to their room.

4 Right after the fall, Roy passed someone in the hallway, and told him that Thomas had stood on a chair and tried to close the window and fell.

5 Some said Roy used drugs, and Roy had been warned not to drink so much.

6 Some said both men liked the same woman.

We know that Roy Ford committed suicide. But we don't know why. And we don't know why Thomas Mullaly fell out of the window.

If you had been the investigator, what kind of questions would you have asked?

Soldiers lined up near the dock; Building 64 is in the background.

BRAVE BABE

PROVES HER POINT

In 1933, skinny, spunky, eighteen-year-old Babe Scott had something to prove.

In fact, she had two things to prove.

Babe had lived on Alcatraz Island for some time. The island was a military prison at the time, and her father was an army sergeant stationed on the island. Sadly, she had just found out that she would not be living in her home on Alcatraz Island much longer.

The government had decided to turn the island into a super-max prison for the "worst of the worst."

The people of San Francisco were afraid they would soon have the country's scariest criminals as neighbors, but the government told them again and again to not worry.

"It's impossible to escape from Alcatraz," the officials announced. "No one can make that swim."

Babe thought she could do it. And in the summer of 1933, she had something else to prove. Babe was a dedicated and talented swimmer, and she hoped to be able to compete for the United States in the 1936 Olympics. But her doctor had told her she had to give up swimming forever. He told her she was too small and skinny—that she wasn't healthy enough.

Babe thought she could prove two things at once. She called a family friend, a captain in the fire department, and asked if he'd watch over her as she took a short swim in the bay. Babe normally swam in a pool, and though her friend was surprised, he went along with it. He rowed a small wooden boat from San Francisco to Alcatraz and watched as she jumped in the water.

And then she struck out for San Francisco!

No woman had ever managed to successfully make this swim. People thought it couldn't be done. But Babe persisted and was triumphant, stepping out of the cold water and up onto the beach at Aquatic Park forty-five minutes later.

Babe's feat made newspaper headlines across the country. Little Babe had proved that Alcatraz was not escape-proof!

She was offered $24,000 to go on a tour around the country for a year, talking to people about her feat. That's equal to almost a half-million dollars today!

But little Babe had big dreams and big convictions. She wanted to go to college to study journalism. She wanted to compete in the 1936 Olympics. If she took the job and the money, she could not do either, at least not right away.

Did waiting pay off for Babe? Not exactly. In 1936, she was not good enough to compete in the Olympics. By 1938, she had gone to college, but she was not a journalist and she was making $94 a month. But Babe never lost her spunk. "Of course, I wouldn't mind some of that money I turned down," Babe sighed.

"But, gosh, I had a lot of high ideals."

USP
ALCATRAZ

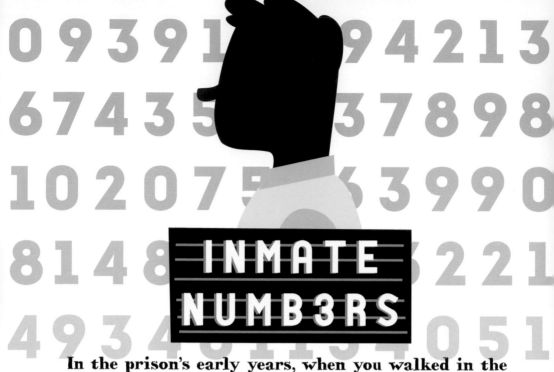

INMATE NUMB3RS

In the prison's early years, when you walked in the door of Alcatraz, you left your name behind.

Inmates might call you by your name or a nickname, but from then on, the guards referred to you only by your number.

How did they decide what number to give you? Simple: you were given the next number on the list. For instance, if you walked in the door directly after Al Capone, you were given the number AZ-86, because Big Al was number AZ-85. The real number AZ-86 was given to a prisoner named William Carter. (AZ was the abbreviation for Alcatraz.) The later you came to the prison, the higher your number.

Still, Alcatraz is a complicated place, and its numbering system wasn't without complications. For instance, when the federal prison opened, there were already 32 inmates in its cells. These men were left behind by the army. Frank Bolt was inmate number AZ-01. So though a man named Frederick White was the first prisoner brought to USP Alcatraz, he was assigned inmate number AZ-33.

Another Alcatraz puzzle: 1,576 numbers were given out, but there were not 1,576 inmates. How can this be?

Some inmates were transferred off Alcatraz, got into more trouble, were sent back, and were given a new number! Thirty-two inmates were locked up on Alcatraz more than once. (Blackie

Audett returned to Alcatraz three times, and had three different numbers: AZ-208, AZ-551, and AZ-1217.)

To make it more complicated, at least two inmates were never given official numbers. Instead, they received the unofficial numbers of A1 and F4. Researchers think that there were 1,544 inmates on Alcatraz during its twenty-nine years of operation as a federal penitentiary. Perhaps later, more unofficial inmates will be discovered and that number will change.

People are superstitious about numbers. The number 666 is considered to be a bad one because in the Bible, it's called "the number of the Beast," or devil. Alcatraz inmate number 666 was a man named William Radkay. When he left prison, he wrote a book titled *The Devil Incarnate: From Altar Boy to Alcatraz.*

Prisoners arriving at Alcatraz.

MUGSHOTS

Mickey Cohen

If you're arrested, you'll end up being photographed.

You'll get a face-on shot, a profile shot, and a number. Your name doesn't matter; you're now just a number in the system.

Al Capone

Thomas Holden

"Mug" is an old word for "face." The first mug shots were on "wanted" posters for Wild West bank robbers.

It's interesting to look at mug shots. Some of the men look sad, some look smug, others look simply confused.

STRANGE
BUT TRUE

Some prisons saved on film—which was expensive—by taking only one photo, using a mirror to create the profile shot.

ALCATRAZ
NICKNAMES

Chances are, you know someone with a nickname.

Many Alcatraz prisoners had nicknames. (Most likely, the other inmates didn't know their true names.)

"Blackie," "Whitey," "Red," and "Curly" were common nicknames that described their owners' hair.

It's easy to imagine why someone would be called "Fatman" or "Slim," "Sailor" or "Soldier." Others are harder to figure out. Tomoya Kawakita was called "Meatball" because he was Japanese, and the Japanese flag has a big red circle on a white background. The red circle represents the sun, but inmates thought it looked like a meatball. "Creepy" Karpis was said to creep around on his toes, and "Quack Quack" liked to make that sound while in his cell. But we'll probably never know why men were nicknamed "Shortgrass," "Grasshopper," or "Beefstew."

Nicknames can often be cruel. But most criminals don't have any problem with being cruel!

PERCY GEARY
AZ-456

ANGEL FACE

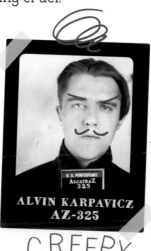

ALVIN KARPAVICZ
AZ-325

CREEPY

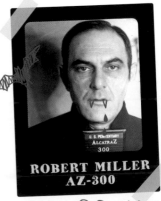

ROBERT MILLER
AZ-300

THE COUNT

WILLIAM VASILICK
AZ-614

WILDMAN

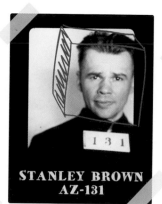

STANLEY BROWN
AZ-131

BOXHEAD

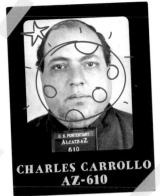

CHARLES CARROLLO
AZ-610

MOONFACE☆

QUACKQUACK

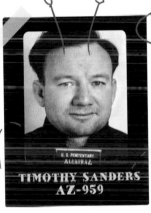

TIMOTHY SANDERS
AZ-959

GRASSHOPPER

GEORGE SINK
AZ-414

WILLIAM MONTGOMERY
AZ-509

PINHEAD

SQUAWK!

TOMOYA KAWAKITA
AZ-1059

MEATBALL

JAMES WALSH
AZ-43

THE PARROT

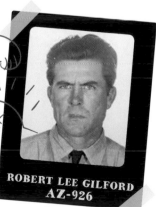

ROBERT LEE GILFORD
AZ-926

BIGSY

35

FATHER DAMIEN'S
Disembodied Hand

MOLOKAI, HAWAII

How are the Hawaiian Islands and Alcatraz Island connected?

By a saint, a dead inmate, and some dirty laundry.

In the mid-1800s, a priest from Belgium made a brave decision. There was a leper colony on the island of Molokai, one of the Hawaiian Islands. Leprosy (which is now called Hansen's Disease) can cause terrible disfigurement to the skin, hands, and feet. Nowadays, there are treatments, but long ago, there was no cure, and leprosy could be caught from someone else. People were so afraid of catching leprosy that they made lepers live far away from everyone, in colonies, where they would suffer on their own.

The priest, Father Damien, knew that lepers needed care and housing, and they needed a priest. So he moved to Molokai to work among them, even though he thought he would eventually catch the disease.

And he did. Father Damien died on the island of Molokai in 1889.

For many years, his grave was visited by the grateful people of Hawaii. But in 1936, the country of Belgium decided that they wanted Father Damien's body.

Despite the cries of the Hawaiian people, the body of their beloved priest was dug up and put on a ship to be returned to the country of his birth.

The ship crossed the ocean and made what they thought would be a quick stop in San Francisco on their way to the Panama Canal. At the Panama Canal, they were to pass the casket to a Belgium ship, which was waiting for it. Father Damien's casket was brought to shore for a day in San Francisco and laid in St. Mary's Cathedral, where hundreds of people paid their respects.

The ship's laundry was sent to Alcatraz Island to be washed. This was one of the jobs that inmates did. But they were on strike. They were angry about the death of an inmate, and refused to work. Because the inmates refused to do the dirty laundry, the ship couldn't leave!

On the other side of the Panama Canal, the Belgium ship waited and waited . . . all because of angry Alcatraz inmates. Finally, the laundry done, Father Damien's casket was loaded back on the ship and sailed through the Panama Canal.

Father Damien was laid to rest in Belgium. The Hawaiian people, however, never stopped lamenting the loss of their beloved priest. They wanted his body returned.

In 1995, Pope John Paul II made a decision. He would bestow the bones of Father Damien's right hand on the Hawaiian people.

So all of Father Damien—except one hand—is buried in Belgium. His right hand rests on the other side of the world, in his old gravesite on Molokai.

In 2009, Father Damien was declared a saint. His life is celebrated by the Hawaiian people on April 15, and many people visit the grave of his right hand.

Will Father Damien's body and hand ever be reunited?

Roy Gardner

THE CONVICT WHO EXECUTED HIMSELF

Some people seem born to be stars, and Roy Gardner was a criminal superstar.

However, history tells us that stars often come to sad, lonely, and tragic ends.

When Roy was a young lawbreaker, everyone knew his name, and his nicknames: The Smiling Bandit. The Last of the Mail Train Robbers. King of the Escape Artists.

Roy was proud that he never fired a gun during a crime. In fact, he tried to make people feel less afraid. He told them he wouldn't hurt them. Of course, he said this as he was pointing a deadly weapon at them and taking their money!

And he was always smiling, even when he got arrested. He treated his criminal career like a game.

Roy excelled at escape. Time and again, he slipped away, dodged, bolted, and fled, but he was always recaptured. Reporters loved him. His exciting exploits sold newspapers. He even used to write to reporters, giving them details to spice up their articles!

One time, Roy was robbing a mail train. He had done this before. But this time was different. The guard in this mail train fought back. He jumped Roy, and they started to fight over the gun. As they were rolling around, Roy suddenly realized two things: First, that one of them could end up dead; he never planned on that! Second, as he said later, "I realized I was a two-bit bum, and the man fighting me was a hard-working man and a hero." Quickly, Roy rolled as far away as he could, put up his hands, and gave up. That way, no one got hurt.

Roy was a complicated man. On the one hand, he loved his wife Dolly and their daughter. On the other, he kept committing crimes that put him in prison and kept him away from his family.

Finally, Roy was sent to Alcatraz with a long sentence. Once there, he realized he had finally made the worst mistake of his life. He would never escape from Alcatraz. He could only see his wife through a tiny window for a half-hour once a month. He could not see his daughter until she was all grown up. Roy told his wife to forget about him, to divorce him and get remarried, and try to keep his life a secret from their daughter. She did this.

For the first time, Roy stopped trying to escape. He followed all the rules in the prison. In the end, he only spent four years at Alcatraz before he was set free. But his wife and daughter were gone forever.

Roy decided to "go straight." He would only make money the honest way. But he found this hard to do. He wrote a book he titled *Hellcatraz*, and at the 1939 World's Fair on Treasure Island, he had a booth: "Crime Does Not Pay!" Sadly, the fairgoers did not pay to see him. Roy grew poor, sick, and sad.

Life was so hard for Roy that he decided he couldn't go on living.

At that time, executions were carried out in a gas chamber. Roy went to a hotel room, and made his own "gas chamber." He mixed chemicals in the sink, then put his head over the sink, covered it with a towel, and breathed in the poisonous gas the chemicals created. He was probably dead within minutes.

Before he did this, he put a note on his hotel door: "Do not open this door. Poison gas. Call police." He didn't want the hotel maid to be poisoned when she came to clean his room.

You might think Roy would write his suicide note to his wife or daughter, or to a close friend. Instead, he addressed it to reporters. "Please let me down as light as possible, boys," he wrote. He also asked them to keep any word of his family a secret.

Did Roy's daughter ever find out her dad was king of the escape artists?

SPANISH DUNGEONS

Alcatraz inmates feared being banished below ground to the dark, dank, and lonely "Spanish Dungeons."

Were these dungeons real? Or just something made up by the guards to scare the inmates?

They were real, all right, but they weren't built by the Spanish. As far as we know, the Spanish sailed into San Francisco Bay in 1775 but never set foot on Alcatraz Island. Why would they? It was a barren rock in the bay, covered in bird poop and seabirds. Some people like to think that the Spanish built tunnels all over the island and buried treasure. But why would they go to the trouble to hack tunnels into a bare rock, when there were so many good and easy hiding places elsewhere? Take Angel Island, for example. It's only two miles away; thirty-five times larger than Alcatraz; covered with hills and valleys, dirt and plants, nooks and crannies; and ringed with beaches. Why not bury or hide something there?

By 1860, the United States Army had built a brick citadel on top of Alcatraz Island. That citadel had one story below ground, surrounded by a moat. When the army decided to build the prison, they knocked down the citadel—all of it except the below-ground section. They constructed the prison building on top of it, and left what remained of the citadel as a kind of basement.

The citadel was surrounded by a dry moat, and on the outer edge of that moat were eight brick storage rooms.

The army put barred doors on these storage rooms and used them as handy places to punish prisoners.

Prisoners in these cells were left alone, far away from everyone. Some prisoners were kept in pitch dark for nineteen days, with only a bucket of water, a bucket for a toilet, and a thin mattress. The prisoners could yell all they wanted: no one would hear.

Not only that, but some of the walls and floors were wet, rough, and slimy. Behind some of the walls were cisterns, water storage areas that look like swimming pools. The water from the cisterns would leak through the brick.

The Alcatraz "dungeons," May 1933.

These cells, called "lower solitary," were used until 1939, when the director of the Bureau of Prisons told the warden to stop using them. The warden had the guards knock down the walls, leaving open alcoves. No one knows what they did with the bars from the doors and windows. Perhaps they threw them in the bay.

Today, these lonely punishment cells, etched with prisoner graffiti, still exist beneath the cellhouse. Desperate prisoners scratched their prisoner numbers into the walls. Sometimes they put tick marks on the walls so they could keep track of how many days they endured in the dark, lonely pit.

How long would you last in a lonely cell, in total darkness. Days? Minutes?

STRANGE BUT TRUE

When D Block, the new solitary unit, was built, massive steel double doors were set into the floor, covering the staircase that led to "the Spanish Dungeons." Inmates watched guards lead prisoners down those stairs, but they never saw them return. The prisoners in solitary didn't know that there was a second set of stairs leading out on the other side of the prison.

THE YOUNGEST INMATE THE CHOCTAW KID

Inmate Clarence Vincent Carnes (AZ-714) was known as the "Choctaw Kid" because he was a Choctaw Indian from Oklahoma.

Clarence arrived at Alcatraz at the age of eighteen, the youngest inmate ever.

But even at his young age, he already knew a lot about prison. When he was only sixteen, he shot a garage attendant to death during a hold-up. He was sent to Granite Reformatory with a life sentence, but escaped and was caught. Then he was sent to Leavenworth Prison in Kansas. When he tried to escape from there, he earned himself a ticket to California—and Alcatraz.

Less than a year after he arrived at Alcatraz, a violent prison riot broke out that was later called "the Battle of Alcatraz."

Clarence Carnes, 1945

Clarence Carnes and five other prisoners took part in it. The prisoners gained control of the prison. They were now in charge! They put officers into cells and shot at them, killing one officer in cold blood. Three of the men trying to escape and another officer were also killed during the battle.

After the riot, Clarence and the two surviving prisoners went on trial for murdering the officers.

The two other prisoners were sentenced to death in the gas chamber

at San Quentin. But Clarence's life was spared. Perhaps it was because of his young age. Perhaps it was because at his trial, guards said that Clarence had done a good thing. During the riot, Clarence had secretly protected the lives of some officers.

Despite being convicted of three murders, Clarence did not spend all of his life in prison. He was paroled at the age of 46.

He was even hired by Hollywood to help make a movie—*Six Against the Rock*—about the Battle of Alcatraz.

But Clarence never learned to follow rules and laws, and eventually, was sent back to prison.

Clarence Carnes, no longer the "young kid," died in prison at the age of 61. He was interred in a pauper's grave.

STRANGE
BUT TRUE

Former Alcatraz inmate Whitey Bulger (AZ-1428) had Clarence's body dug up, placed in a $4,000 copper coffin, and reburied on Indian land in Oklahoma.

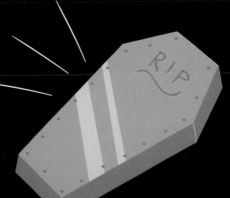

FIVE THEORIES

When we read prison escape stories, or watch them on TV or in the movies, we're always hoping the prisoner makes it. If we don't like crime, why are we on the side of the criminal?

① We believe what we see in the movies. Movies with prison escapes generally have this combination: An innocent man who is:

    a. handsome, likeable, and smart,
    b. surrounded by stupid, violent criminals, and
    c. abused by a cruel guard.

Of course, we want the prisoner to escape!

② We like scary things, as long as they're not real. When we play video games, we pretend to do frightening things we would never do in our real lives.

    In pictures or videos of prisoners, they often don't look dangerous or cruel. We can't imagine them doing horrible, violent things to people. It's painful for us to think of the victims and what happened to them, so we don't.

A prisoner can come across as nice and funny, someone we'd like to be friends with. Of course, we want the prisoner to escape!

③ We all have a bit of the rebel in us. The prisoner sometimes seems much like us, except he lives a more exciting life. He seems brave, and he takes risks. Maybe, for just a moment, we want to be a bit like him. Of course, we want him to escape!

④ We love an underdog. We root for him to win. Of course, we want the prisoner to escape!

⑤ We all want to escape from something. We all want to be free of something. Perhaps when we see an escape movie, we remember what we feel imprisoned by. It might be something basic, like poverty or a bully at school. Maybe we want to be free from an annoying brother or sister. Maybe we just want to be free of doing chores. There's always something we yearn to be free of. Maybe when we root for a prisoner, we're rooting for the part of us that wants to leave a problem in our lives far, far behind. Of course, we want the prisoner to escape!

But let's look at the facts. It's late at night, and you're home asleep, safe in your bed. Suddenly, your bedroom window is shattered and moments later, a large, menacing figure is standing over you.

Now do you wish the prisoner had escaped?

THE *SHORTEST* ESCAPE

It's hard to say who, exactly, had the shortest escape. About ten inmates managed to escape just as far as the edge of the island before being caught. One of them was John Bayless (AZ-466), who made it into the water for just a few minutes.

In 1941, John Bayless was on garbage detail, which actually was a coveted job. He got to work outside in the fresh air, overlooking the beautiful bay. All he had to do was pick up trash and do odd jobs. A guard stood nearby.

One afternoon, the shoreline was blanketed with a thick fog.

Without much thought, Bayless took advantage of it by jumping into the water. He certainly didn't spend a lot of time planning his escape!

Bayless surely must have gasped when he plunged into the cold water. He would have watched the island sweep past as he was dragged by the unrelenting current. The fog was so thick he couldn't see much of anything. He'd never make it to shore! Immediately, he realized his mistake. He was probably relieved when he was captured and brought back to the Rock.

Of course, John Bayless was punished for his escape attempt and had to serve more years. But he wasn't done making bad decisions. A little over a year later, he went on trial in San Francisco. While in the courthouse, he suddenly broke away from the US Marshal who was guarding him and made a dash to freedom.

He was not successful. For his foolish escape attempts, he was sentenced to serve thirty more years in prison. Perhaps he should have given it a bit more thought.

Like many inmates, John Bayless was a man without a plan. After all, no one plans to spend all of his life in prison. And yet that's what John Bayless did.

Bayless went into and out of prison repeatedly; in fact, he even left and returned to Alcatraz. The most time he spent outside of prison at one time was four months.

He ended up dying in prison as a broken, sick old man. Bayless was not the first man to start off young and hopeful only to go downhill, year after wasted year. The photos show the toll prison took on Bayless's body and spirit.

1943

1945

1952

1974

THE LONGEST ESCAPE

Was inmate John Paul Scott (AZ-1403) the luckiest man alive, or the unluckiest?

Scott's long criminal career—along with his daring escape attempts—landed him a stay at "inescapable" Alcatraz. Eventually, Scott was assigned a job in the basement area below the kitchen, where he prepared vegetables for the cooks. Soon, he realized he'd stumbled into a lucky situation.

A single guard had to keep track of not only the basement workers but also, the kitchen workers on the floor above, and Scott was often left unwatched. Whenever he could, he checked the bars on the windows, searching every nook and cranny to see if there might be any place, any way that he could break his way out of the prison.

Lucky Scott! He came upon some window bars that other inmates had cut away at for months before being transferred. All he had to do was make the cuts deeper.

Eventually, on December 16, 1962, Scott was ready to make a break for it. He asked another inmate, Darl Dee Parker (AZ-1413), if he wanted to go along. The two men waited until a guard checked on them at 5:20 p.m.

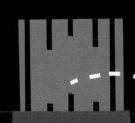

Then, after he went upstairs, Scott and Parker broke out the bars using a long piece of wood as a lever, then broke the glass and shoved through the small opening and out the window. Scott also carried pieces of a prison shirt, a few rubber gloves, and a long electrical cord with him.

They were out! Now what? They were on the west side of the prison building and planned to enter the water on the opposite side (facing San Francisco). So, instead of running around the building, they climbed a pipe three stories up to the prison roof.

They then ran across the roof and, using the electrical cord, lowered themselves down the far wall. Once on the ground again, they scrambled down the cliff to the water.

Scott blew up the gloves like balloons, tied them off, stuffed them into the sleeves of the extra prison shirt, and knotted it around him like a kind of swim floatie.

Unluckily for Scott and Parker, they entered the bay on an outgoing tide—the water was rushing hard and fast toward the ocean. Making it even harder, the sun had just set and it was dark.

As soon as Parker stepped into the water, he was in trouble, tumbled head over heels by the choppy waves.

He even lost his false teeth! Gasping for breath, he splashed to a nearby rock called "Little Alcatraz." Only a few minutes before, he'd hoped to leave Alcatraz forever. Now he clung to the little rock and hoped that someone would find him and take him back to the island! His wish was soon granted.

Meanwhile, John Paul Scott paddled furiously toward the lights of San Francisco, but that same cold current carried him away from the shore and toward the Golden Gate Bridge. If he went under the bridge, he'd end up in the Pacific Ocean. He'd never survive that! He might even become a shark's tasty meal.

Meanwhile, he was getting colder and colder. His fingers, his hands, even his arms and legs stopped responding. As his body temperature dropped, it became harder and harder to move . . . to think.

Bam! Bam! Floundering in the black water, he was slammed against the sharp rocks at the south end of the Golden Gate Bridge.

The violent waves had torn off his clothes. He was naked except for his socks. He wanted to pull himself onto the rocks, but none of his limbs were working. Then he passed out, and a wave picked him up and deposited him on the rocks.

Scott had made it! He done what everyone said wasn't possible! He had escaped the Rock.

Or had he? Scott was dying, his body shutting down from the cold. Would you call that an escape?

Once again, Scott was lucky. Two teenagers saw him on the rocks and notified the Presidio's military police, who arrived along with the army's fire department. At first, the rescuers thought Scott was dead, but then he began to stir. They pulled Scott off the rocks and took him to the army hospital at the Presidio. For a while, doctors weren't sure they could save Scott, but eventually, they managed to warm him up.

Bashed and battered, Scott was returned that same evening to the island prison he had left just hours before. He had made it three miles from Alcatraz. In the photos taken of him at the hospital, Scott is smirking.

Other escapees—Theodore Cole, Ralph Roe, Frank Morris, the Anglin brothers—may have made it farther, but we'll never know for sure because they were never found (either alive or dead). What we do know is that John Paul Scott put three miles between himself and the prison island.

At least for a moment, Scott was the luckiest man alive!

THE MOST
(IN)FAMOUS INMATE

AL CAPONE

Ask any American, "Who's the most famous gangster of all?" and the answer you'll most likely get is "Al Capone!"

Every day at Alcatraz, thousands of visitors look up at drab little cell 181 on B Block, trying to imagine one of the most powerful men in United States criminal history trapped in that tiny pen. Capone—also known as "Scarface"—was an underworld giant who fell to the level of a caged rat.

In the 1920s, Chicago was plagued by violent gang wars. The sound of tommy-gun fire seemed to hang in the air over the city. In just a few years, almost 400 gangsters were killed by other gangsters, or by the police. Citizens were outraged. Everyone knew that Capone was the most powerful, obscenely rich, and ruthless gangster in Chicago, but no one could do anything about it. He seemed to be untouchable by the law.

Capone worked his gang like a business, and he had good business sense. It was said that at one time, he was worth $300 million! (That's about $4 billion in today's money.)

He used three basic tools: minions, payoffs, and threats.

He never did the "dirty work" himself. He had dozens, perhaps hundreds, of minions to do it for him.

If, for instance, a big jewel heist was going down, his minions made sure that crooked policemen had been bribed to "look the other way." What did they do about the honest cops, the ones who couldn't be bought? They threatened. If the honest cop didn't do what Capone wanted . . . well, let's just say that someone might get hurt or turn up dead. It might be the cop, or (they'd tell him), it might be his wife, his children, his brother, his mother.

It's easy to control people with fear. What Capone wanted, Capone got.

With enough minions, bribes, and threats, Capone soon ran the city of Chicago. Later he expanded. He controlled state judges, prosecutors, and police as well. How could he be stopped?

In 1930, the man who headed the Chicago Crime Commission came up with an idea: a list of the worst criminals. He called it the list of "Public Enemies," and Al Capone was named "Public Enemy Number One." People loved the sound of that. It was printed in newspapers all over the United States. (In fact, the term is still

used to this day.)

The federal government took notice. Who was this ultra-rich Capone gangster in Chicago who was snubbing his nose at rules and regulations? And how could he be stopped?

One day, someone thought of a way: taxes.

Americans pay taxes on money they've earned. Someone looked at Capone's tax forms, on which he claimed that he earned only a few thousand dollars each year. Everyone knew that wasn't true. Capone was rolling in dough.

The government came down hard on Al Capone. It didn't matter that he made this money illegally. The Feds said that however a person made money, taxes had to be paid on it. It turned out to be easy to prove that Capone hadn't paid his full share of taxes.

As always, Capone thought he could weasel, threaten, and charm his way out of trouble. But now he was playing with the Feds. And the Feds played by their rules, not Capone's.

Capone entered Alcatraz just like any other prisoner. He wasn't even "Mr. Capone" anymore. He was plain AZ-85. It took a few months, but eventually, even he had to admit his reign was over. He said, "It looks like Alcatraz has got me licked."

Scarface: the most wealthy, powerful, ruthless gangster ever to walk the streets of Chicago. Brought down by the Internal Revenue Service.

Early Alcatraz inmates lived a very strict life, cut off from their families and friends. They could only receive and send a few letters every month. Not only that, when they wrote a letter, they couldn't put it in an envelope and mail it. They had to give it to a guard. The guard typed the letter on a typewriter, using slightly different words to make sure an inmate couldn't pass along a message in a code.

For instance, if an inmate wrote,

LET TOMMY KNOW HOW MUCH I MISS HIM AND THAT I HOPE HE HAS A GOOD BIRTHDAY PARTY

the guard might type only,

HAPPY BIRTHDAY TO TOM.

But prisoners have always been crafty and sneaky and creative. Inmates were allowed to read some magazines, and there was a way they could use them to receive a coded message.

Before a magazine was given to a prisoner, one of the

guards would check it and tear out any pages that might have information a prisoner might want (such as how to make something that might help him escape). But some inmates could receive codes in an ad. Most magazines, even today, have small ads in the back. Before the Internet, magazine ads were important ways for people to sell all sorts of things.

What kind of message was being passed through an ad like this one?

MISS BESSIE WHITE
of P.O. Box 133, Sausalito,
is selling a red fishing boat
for **$500**.
You can see the boat during
April at 300 Northwest Drive
from **12 noon to 4 pm**.

Here's what the ad is really saying:

If your relatives send **$500** to **MISS BESSIE WHITE** of P.O. Box 133, Sausalito, a red fishing boat will be waiting for you from **12 noon to 4 pm** 300 yards to the Northwest of Alcatraz Island every day during the month of April.

If your relatives or friends send the money to "Miss Bessie White," you might have a chance to escape. All you'd have to do is get past the guards at your work assignment, past the guards in the gun towers, over the fence, down the cliff into the water, and swim 300 yards without being spotted!

CONTRABAND

Everyone likes to hide things—to have secrets.

We also know this can get us into trouble.

This is especially true in prison, where you'll be punished for having contraband, which is anything you're not allowed to have. In prison, that item could be as deadly as a prisoner-made knife, called a "shiv" or "shank," or as innocent as an extra library book.

Correctional officers were kept busy looking for contraband; they often did cell shakedowns to make sure the inmates were not hiding anything. What tedious work! The guards had to pick up and examine each and every little item in an inmate's cell. After all, an inmate could easily slip a razor into a book, or a wiggle a rusty, sharpened piece of metal into his mattress, then use it against an officer.

Lethal shivs and shanks were the most common contraband items. But at Alcatraz, prisoners also smuggled and hid food. At most prisons, inmates are able to buy things like candy or cookies at the prison commissary (store). But there was no commissary at Alcatraz, so they would smuggle food from the dining hall. They could be thrown in the hole (solitary) if they were caught with cake in their cells!

It's strange to think, but even the hardest criminals loved sweets, and were willing to risk punishment to get them.

STRANGE BUT TRUE

Inmate Robert Moxon (AZ-34) spent time in the isolation unit for smuggling a rubber duckie into his cell!

OLD SPARKY

If you visit Alcatraz, do they let you see the electric chair?

No, because there was never an electric chair at Alcatraz.

Most executions are done in state prisons, and Alcatraz was a federal (US) prison.

The federal government doesn't do many executions. Execution chambers are expensive to build. They only make sense if you're going to use them.

The first federal execution in the United States happened in 1790, but the first federal execution chamber wasn't built until 1995, more than 200 years later. It's at the Federal Correctional Complex in Terre Haute, Indiana. The first inmate executed there was Timothy McVeigh, known as the Oklahoma City Bomber.

Before that, federal prisoners were sent to a state prison to be executed.

Three Alcatraz inmates were executed, all by lethal gas. Two of them were Sam Shockley and Miran Thompson, who took part in a prison riot that happened at Alcatraz in 1946. They were tried and convicted of being involved in the killing of a prison guard during this riot, although the inmate who actually shot the guard (and others held hostage in the cells) had died during the riot.

The third was perhaps the worst Alcatraz inmate: Billy Cook (AZ-918). He went on a crime spree and kidnapped and murdered a mom, a dad, and their three children, who were seven, four, and three years old, and even their dog. He dumped all of the bodies in an old mine shaft. He was executed in 1952.

STRANGE BUT TRUE

Alcatraz inmates Sam Shockley and Miran Thompson were executed side-by-side in the San Quentin State Prison gas chamber.

SHARKS!

Is San Francisco Bay teeming with ferocious predators ready to tear off a swimmer's legs?

The guards at Alcatraz certainly wanted the inmates to believe it was. After all, it would make their jobs easier. Why would a prisoner try to break out knowing he could end up in the razor-sharp teeth of a great white shark?

During the time Alcatraz was a military prison, hundreds of men worked outside. One day, they planned a mass escape. After all, if everyone jumped into the bay at once, it would be difficult to catch most of them. Then the commander of Alcatraz, Colonel Cralle, called them to attention, and told them, "Go ahead! Swim!" Perhaps thinking of the sharks they'd been warned about, the men went back to work.

It's generally believed that great white sharks don't often venture too far into San Francisco Bay. In modern times, there are no reports of a great white attack on a human in the bay, even though thousands of swimmers have taken part in races between Alcatraz and the city.

Recently, scientists put electronic tags on 179 great whites near the Pacific Ocean's Farallon Islands, about thirty miles from Alcatraz. This is called the "Red Triangle" because about 11 percent of all shark attacks worldwide happen in this area. Tagging the sharks allowed the scientists to see where the great whites traveled. What they discovered is that they swam thousands of miles, mainly to two areas: Hawaii or a spot in the mid-Pacific that the scientists named "the Shark Café."

They also discovered that seven of these sharks swam into San Francisco Bay, but they don't believe they went far. Why don't great whites fill the bay? After all, it's full of sea lions and seals— delicious meals!

Scientists aren't sure, but they think these sharks try to avoid two things. One is the bay's strong currents. The other is the fresh water that enters the bay from the rivers that empty into it. The bay is not as salty as the ocean. Great whites want to live in saltwater.

Yet the bay is teeming with sharks! There are about eleven types in the bay, with such interesting names as brown smoothhound, sevengill, cowshark, soupfin, cookiecutter and spiny dogfish. Luckily for swimmers, these sharks don't eat people. They're actually quite shy, and stay close to the bottom of the bay, where they feed on fish and crabs.

There may have been plenty of things for inmates to fear during an escape, but great white sharks were not among them.

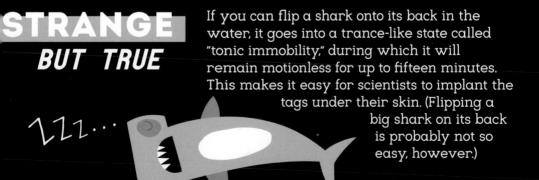

STRANGE
BUT TRUE

Zzz...

If you can flip a shark onto its back in the water, it goes into a trance-like state called "tonic immobility," during which it will remain motionless for up to fifteen minutes. This makes it easy for scientists to implant the tags under their skin. (Flipping a big shark on its back is probably not so easy, however.)

THE MOST HATED
CON ON ALCATRAZ

Rufe Persful (AZ-284) was the most hated con on Alcatraz. Other cons wanted him dead. He had to look over his shoulder every minute of every day. Was it because he had murdered a man? No, the inmates had no problems with that. It was because he'd break the "convict code" and help out the guards if he got something good out of it.

He was a squealer and a snitch—the worst thing you can be in prison.

And yet, he asked to be sent to Alcatraz. What was his story?

At eighteen years old, Rufe Persful robbed and killed an elderly man and was sent to Tucker Prison Farm in Arkansas. At this prison, prisoners had to work all day long in hot fields. Since they were working outside in a large area, the prison needed a lot of guards to watch over them, more guards than they had. One way they could make up the difference was to turn a prisoner into a type of guard called a **"trusty."** They even gave him a gun.

Not only that, the trusty could get out of prison early if he stopped another inmate from escaping.

Rufe became a trusty. If you were in Tucker Prison Farm, you'd certainly quickly learn to never turn your back on Rufe Persful—he might shoot you and say you were running away.

No surprise, Persful did shoot a fellow inmate, and was rewarded by being let out of prison.

But Rufe was a violent man, and he committed another crime, shooting a woman in the back. He was sent back to Tucker, and, amazingly, was made a trusty once again. Again, he shot an escaping convict, and was released.

Yes, all of it happened a third time! Rufe got out of prison, committed another crime, and was put back in. But this time, he wasn't sent to Tucker. He was sent to the federal prison in Atlanta. This was the worst thing that could happen to Rufe. At Atlanta, he was just another con, not a trusty on a horse, wielding a gun.

And the other cons knew his story.

Rufe was constantly threatened; finally, he was held down and beaten with a hammer. Afterward, he begged the warden to send him to Alcatraz.

He thought that at Alcatraz, he could have a fresh start. No one would know his story.

He was transferred, but his happiness didn't last long. His story arrived before he did. Every day on the Rock could be Rufe's last. He begged to be sent to yet another prison. But he had made a mistake. Many wanted to leave Alcatraz, but precious few did. Rufe was stuck on the Rock. He had to think of a way off, a way no one else had tried. And finally, he did.

One day, while working near the fire engine, he suddenly grabbed the fire ax from its holder. He put his left hand on the hood of the engine and chopped off all but his thumb. Then he handed the ax to fellow inmate Homer Parker (AZ-334) and asked him to "finish the job" by cutting off his right hand. Of course, Parker did no such thing.

Even this didn't get him off the island. He spent six months in the Alcatraz hospital, where he slowly went crazy. At last, he was transferred to the hospital for federal prisoners at Springfield, Illinois, and there, regained his sanity.

Once again, Rufe was transferred, this time to the federal penitentiary at McNeil Island, Washington. Though his life was threatened there as well, he survived six years, and was paroled.

Finally, he could run away from his past and his story! He moved in with his brother in Indiana. Then he got married and lived an almost normal life. Almost. He ended up marrying and divorcing four times before he finally died at the ripe old age of 84. What did Rufe tell people in Indiana when they asked about his missing hand? Did he lie and say that it happened in a farming accident?

Or did Rufe Persful 'fess up about Tucker Prison Farm, and Alcatraz, and the flash of a fireman's ax?

FIRST & LAST
INMATES

Frank Bolt was prisoner AZ-01. He had committed his crimes while he was a soldier in Hawaii.

The last inmate was Frank Weatherman, an armed robber. He was assigned the last prison number: AZ-1576. Frank was on the island only a few months.

When the prison closed its doors on March 21, 1963, the island was full of newspaper reporters and photographers, all clamoring to get the best stories and pictures. Only twenty-seven inmates were left; most of the others had already been sent to the new federal super-max prison in Marion, Illinois.

AZ-01

AZ-1576

As the inmates filed out of the cellhouse and onto the prison launch, flashbulbs popped. Many inmates covered their faces. The last inmate checked into the prison was the last to leave: Frank Weatherman.

Reporters love a good quote, and Frank Weatherman gave them one. As he stepped off the island, he said:

"Alcatraz never was no good for nobody!"

THE MAN WHO OUTWITTED MACHINE GUN KELLY

It was late in the evening on July 22, 1933, and a wealthy oilman named Charles Urschel was enjoying a pleasant night, playing cards with his friends on the front porch of his house in Oklahoma City.

Suddenly, two armed men burst onto the porch, shouting. One brandished a deadly tommy gun. Though Urschel didn't know it at the time, that man was Machine Gun Kelly!

The two men kidnapped Urschel and demanded a ransom of $200,000—more than $3.5 million in today's money—to return him to his family. ("Ransom" is money that's paid to have the kidnapped person returned safe and sound.)

In 1933, kidnapping often paid off, and paid off big. Except, this time, it wouldn't.

Machine Gun Kelly had picked the wrong man to snatch. Charles Urschel was not a helpless victim.

Urschel was handcuffed, blindfolded, thrown in the back of a car, and taken for a drive that lasted a couple of hours. Once at the kidnappers' destination, he was locked up in a small, shack-like house; the blindfold and handcuffs stayed on. However, he realized he could use his other senses. For example, when he asked for a drink of water, he noticed the noise of a water pump. He even noticed that the water had a strong mineral taste to it.

Day after day, Urschel languished as the kidnappers tried

to work out a deal for the ransom. But he didn't lose hope, and he kept his wits about him. He heard an airplane fly over the house twice a day. After a while, he began to casually ask his captors what time it was.

He found that he was hearing the plane at 9:45 every morning, and again at 5:45 every night.

Then one day, there was no airplane. What was different? It was raining heavily. Urschel wondered: could a storm be the reason?

He also chatted to his captors as much as he could. They were quite likely bored, and perhaps they liked having Urschel to talk to. He memorized the sound of their voices, and knew they would eventually mess up and give him clues by mistake. And they did. They began to brag about bank robberies they'd pulled. Charles Urschel mentally noted every detail.

Meanwhile, the ransom payoff was not going well. Five days after the kidnapping, Urschel's family was told that if they wanted to see him alive, a family friend named Kirkpatrick was to board a train going to Kansas City, Missouri, at night. He was to look for bonfires on the right side of the train track. When he saw the second one, he was to throw the suitcase full of ransom money out of the train.

Kirkpatrick did as he was told, but there were no bonfires. Had Machine Gun Kelly made a mistake?

Finally, eight days after the kidnapping, the handoff happened in the simplest way possible. Kirkpatrick, who was still in Kansas City, got a phone call telling him to walk down a street near the LaSalle Hotel and hand over the suitcase when asked. Of course, the FBI had recorded the serial numbers on the bills so they could be identified later.

MUNCH MUNCH MUNCH

Machine Gun took the money back to the farm, where it was divided up. Now that the kidnappers had the money, they could do what they wanted. Should they return Urschel, or kill him?

They decided to make good on their deal. They drove Urschel back to Oklahoma. When at long last, his blindfold came off, he was standing in the rain on the side of a road with $10 in his pocket for a taxi—and he was free.

Have you ever heard the saying, "Don't get mad, get even"? This is exactly what Urschel did.

Urschel helped the FBI gather the pieces of the puzzle. By the length of the car ride, they guessed the general area where he had been held. The animal sounds indicated that it was probably a ranch. A ranch would need a pump to get water from the ground, and the water's mineral taste meant he might have been in Texas. When the FBI had narrowed down the location, agents checked all the nearby airports and marked up a map showing where planes would have been in the air every day at precisely 9:45 a.m. and 5:45 p.m. They even discovered a plane that didn't fly one day because of bad weather.

The clever detectives—and Urschel—put it all together and figured out that Urschel had been held at a ranch outside of Paradise, Texas, owned by Machine Gun Kelly's in-laws.

It didn't take the FBI long to find the money, and to find Kelly. Soon after, Machine Gun Kelly became Alcatraz inmate AZ-117.

Charles Urschel had outwitted a big-time gangster. He didn't get mad—he got even.

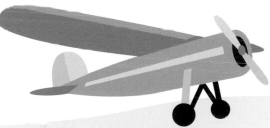

PUT-PUT-PUT-PUT-PUT

DRIP

DRIP

DRIP

THE FOUR STAGES OF DROWNING

① SHOCK

Can you die in just two minutes?

If you're dumped into very cold water, you will automatically take in a huge gasp of air, called the "reflexive gasp." If you're underwater, you will suck cold water into your lungs. That will kill you quickly.

Still, if you're above water when you gasp, you can still die of shock. Water can be so cold it shocks your heart into not beating, or beating with a faulty rhythm. Either way, your brain doesn't get enough oxygen and death comes quickly, usually within the first two minutes.

② SWIM FAILURE

If you don't know how to swim, or get too tired, cold, or scared to swim, you'll sink beneath the waves and get water in your lungs. But oddly, many people who drown don't have water in their lungs. If a person has water in his or her mouth, the larynx will usually close up—after all, you don't drown while drinking a glass of water! But if you pass out, your larynx may stay closed, and you suffocate.

LARYNX

LUNGS

③ HYPOTHERMIA

We all know our bodies like to be 98.6 degrees. If your temperature reaches even a few degrees hotter, you feel miserable. Seven degrees above normal can kill you.

It's the same with cold. In fact, you will begin to die when your body temperature drops by just four or five degrees. To make things worse, if you're in cold water, your arms and legs will stop working. Your body will send much of the blood in your body out of your arms and legs and into your vital organs, making **swim failure** happen faster.

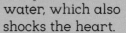

$-98.6°$

$-94°$

④ POST-RESCUE COLLAPSE

Once a person is rescued, they're still not completely safe. In fact, up to 20 percent of people who are rescued later die. They can be awake and talking, then suddenly die! They may have too much water in their lungs, or their heart beats poorly and doesn't recover in time. A person's blood pressure can change rapidly when pulled from the water, which also shocks the heart.

At least four Alcatraz inmates died in the water. None died of post-rescue collapse. What stage did the others perish in? We will never know.

STRANGE
BUT TRUE

Oddly enough, very cold water can also save you from drowning! Cold water makes your heart rate slow down. This actually helps you. People have been people have been rescued after being in very cold water for up to 40 minutes—and survived!

PRISONERS  IN THE

Imagine the inmates bursting into the recreation yard on weekends, like kids to a playground.

They could get fresh air and talk with fellow inmates—maybe plan escapes! And just for a while, they could choose to do what they wanted rather than what they were told.

There's a breathtaking view of the Golden Gate Bridge from the top of the concrete steps on one side of the rec yard, but it's sliced in half by a fence topped with barbed wire. It was a grim reminder to inmates of exactly where they were.

Still, the rec yard was a place to forget their problems and just have fun. Baseball was a favorite game, especially among the younger men. There was one baseball rule that was quite different, however: if you hit the ball over a fence, it was an out, not a home run. After all, no one could jump the fence to get the ball back! In fact, in the early years, they had very few baseballs, and the game would be over for the day if the last one went over the fence.

Can you imagine a yard full of hardened prisoners furious that you were the one who walloped the last ball out of the "park"? But there was one way you could hit the ball outside the

PLAYGROUND

boundaries that everyone loved. If you hit it into left field, you just might break a cellhouse window. The men loved the sound of a crashing window, and would erupt into cheers.

It's possible that the inmates themselves named their teams. A 1938 roster shows four teams in a playoff, named after minor-league teams of the day: the San Francisco Seals, the Oakland Oaks, the Boston Bees, and the Tulsa Oilers.

One of the games the inmates played was horseshoes—yes, violent men were given heavy chunks of iron to play with. Inmates definitely used them as weapons, but, since inmates never "snitched" on each other, if an inmate was hit, he would say it was his fault. The doctor on the island saw many prisoners who said their head got in the way of a tossed horseshoe "by mistake."

However, in 1944, there was a riot in the rec yard, during which there was no denying that the prisoners were bashing each other with horseshoes. That toy was finally taken away from them.

The older inmates loved to play cards, especially the game called bridge. They played behind the baseball backstops. They also loved to play poker, but they weren't allowed to. No gambling! But they would play quick games when the guards weren't watching.

They weren't actually given cards to play with, though, for two reasons: first, the rec yard is always windy, and cards would blow away, and second, playing cards of those days had a cellulose coating, and the cellulose could be scraped off and lit to make a tiny explosion! So the inmates had to use colored dominoes in place of cards.

Despite the fun, the rec yard could be the worst place in the prison. If other inmates were out to get you and you had no friends to watch your back, the rec yard was dangerous. There were usually more than 200 inmates milling around, watched over by only a few guards patrolling the catwalk, and two in the yard.

What could you do if someone was out to get you? You could always follow one of the two guards around and stand close to him. You could always keep your back to the wall. Still, some

inmates were so fearful of what might happen in the yard that they stayed in their cells instead of going out. They were usually very pale, since they never got sunshine.

One more thing you had to watch out for: crossing the "deadline."

In the corners on top of the yard wall were three "birdcages."

These were glass boxes the guards could go into to get out of the bone-chilling wind, but still be able to see the inmates. However, the corners were blind spots. A thick red line was painted on the ground—a deadline. If you crossed it, you might be shot dead!

STRANGE BUT TRUE

In 1938, the "yard bird"—the prisoner who cleaned up the recreation yard after the inmates left—was none other than Big Al Capone!

Prison Recreation Yard.

THE SLAMMER

Boom! Rumble-rumble-rumble-rumble KABLAM!

Nothing says "prison" like the sound of 250 pounds of tool-proof steel slamming shut.

Alcatraz cell doors are the symbol of security. They were designed in 1934 specifically for Alcatraz. The design was so good that it was copied in prisons all over the United States, and is still in use in many of them. Hundreds of thousands of prisoners still hear that foreboding sound, that ominous KABLAM! You may not like the sound of your alarm clock, but it's sweet when compared to the slam of a cell door.

When the Bureau of Prisons took over Alcatraz, the cells still had the old doors of the military prison. These doors were dangerous for officers. Each door swung open like a door in your house (or like a great big, heavy metal weapon). The cell doors had to be opened and closed one at a time, and locked with an individual key while the inmate stood inches away. This would never do for a prison full of "the worst of the worst."

The prisoners really wanted to find out how to control the new doors! But the system was complicated and secured behind locked panels. Every tier and every corner of each cellblock has a control box that protects the mechanism, which can open either thirteen or fourteen cell doors at the same time. The key to the panels was kept by an armed guard, high up in the gun gallery. When it was needed, the gun gallery guard would lower it to the officer on the floor. When he was done, he sent the key back up.

In 1934, this system was considered a new technology, which was called "remote controlled." We think that things that are remote controlled are controlled by radio waves, such as a remote-controlled airplane, or a remote for your TV. But "remote" only means "far away." In this mechanical system, the doors were far away from the control box.

Once officer said that when the prisoners walked in from the recreation yard,

Guard opening cell doors.

he had to watch what they did as they filed by the control box— they would sometimes quietly spit on the indicator handle, and if he didn't pay attention, he might end up with a big gob in his hand!

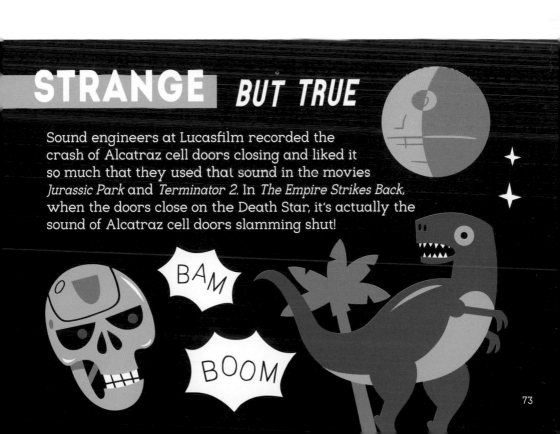

STRANGE BUT TRUE

Sound engineers at Lucasfilm recorded the crash of Alcatraz cell doors closing and liked it so much that they used that sound in the movies *Jurassic Park* and *Terminator 2*. In *The Empire Strikes Back*, when the doors close on the Death Star, it's actually the sound of Alcatraz cell doors slamming shut!

BAM

BOOM

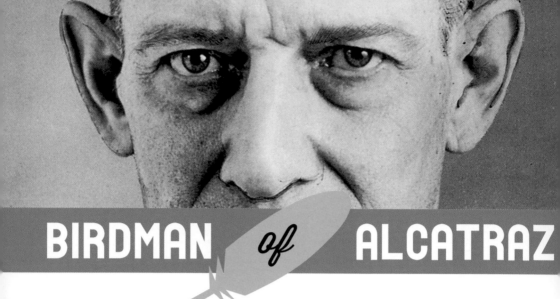

BIRDMAN *of* ALCATRAZ

Women—mothers, daughters, sisters, aunts—seemed to adore Robert Stroud (AZ-594), known as the Birdman of Alcatraz.

How did he get his nickname? Why was a ruthless killer admired by so many normal, law-abiding Americans?

Robert Stroud's criminal life started early, when at 18, he murdered a man in Alaska. He was sentenced to spend 12 years in prison. Stroud was an angry, cold-blooded man. One day, he was written up by a guard for breaking a rule. Because of this, he lost the right to have visitors for a while. When Stroud found out that his brother tried to visit but was turned away, he was vindictive. In the dining hall, Stroud stabbed to death the guard who wrote him up.

He was sentenced to be executed by hanging, but the punishment was changed to life in solitary confinement. This meant he would spend the rest of his days in a cell by himself.

While in prison in US Penitentiary Leavenworth (Kansas), he became interested in birds after making a pet of a wild sparrow. Those who ran USP Leavenworth at the time had some rather odd ideas. Inmates were allowed to do all kinds of things, including operating their own businesses from their cells! Stroud began to buy and sell canaries, and he also began to study them. He wrote a book called *Stroud's Digest on the Diseases of Birds*, which became well known. Eventually, his cell was full of canaries, birds that poop fifty times a day! (Stroud didn't care about cleanliness.)

In the 1920s and 1930s, most Americans lived on farms. County

fairs, which were held once a year, were one of the most important events in people's lives. At these fairs, women entered their best cakes and pies, their roses and quilts, in contests in the hope of winning prize ribbons. They also entered their canaries in warbling contests.

In those days, it was common for housewives to keep canaries in their kitchens to brighten the house with bird song. They read books and magazines about how best to care for and enjoy their canaries. Robert Stroud wrote books and penned many articles and answered the letters of the hundreds of bird-lovers who wrote to him. In fact, he was so busy that a guard was assigned just to take care of his correspondence!

What the women who wrote to him didn't know was that Robert Stroud was a callous killer.

Eventually, one of his fans found out he was in prison, and let everyone know. But she made it sound as if Robert Stroud was a gentle, misunderstood man. After all, he was a bird-lover! Women all over America signed petitions, asking officials to release Robert Stroud from prison. If they only knew the "real" Robert Stroud, they would never have done this. Like many people, they wanted to believe the best. Only prison guards knew this inmate's brutal, egotistical side.

Now, things were really out of control in Leavenworth. The warden had had enough. Lucky for him, there was an answer to all his problems. It was an island in the middle of San Francisco Bay: Alcatraz.

Stroud was sent to the Rock in 1942, and had to leave his birds behind. He was not allowed to have a business, and his letter writing was restricted. Just when it seemed Stroud was to become yet another forgotten inmate, a man named Thomas Gaddis wrote a very sympathetic book.

In his book, Robert Stroud was a kind, gentle bird-lover who had been treated cruelly and unjustly. At first, Gaddis wanted to title the book *Bird Doctor of Leavenworth*, but then thought no one would buy a book with that title.

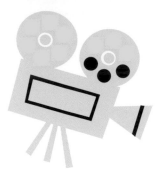

Instead, he came up with the snappy title *Birdman of Alcatraz*, even though Stroud never kept a single bird in his Alcatraz cells, and no one had ever called him "Birdman."

The book flew off the shelves, and soon, a movie was made starring Burt Lancaster. Again, Stroud was depicted as a man of dignity who rose above injustice. Robert Stroud was once again in the limelight. Once again, people who knew nothing of the real man signed petitions to have him released from prison.

Of course, this would never happen. Finally, old and ill, Stroud was transferred to the prison hospital in Missouri, and died there in 1963.

In some ways, it appeared that Robert Stroud lived an exciting life. There was a book! A movie! Thousands of admirers!

Yet he was never allowed to see the movie. He was never allowed to meet a fan. He spent his entire adult life alone, believing himself to be important while looking at nothing but cold, steel walls.

In the play *Romeo and Juliet*, Shakespeare wrote, "What's in a name? That which we call a rose by any other name would smell as sweet." Is that true of Robert Stroud? Not really.

Without his nickname, the "Birdman of Alcatraz" would have been forgotten long ago and Alcatraz would have one less "famous" inmate.

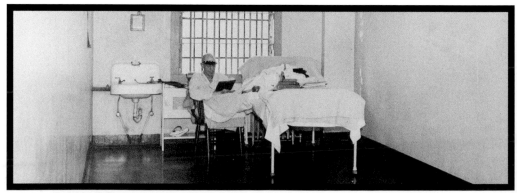

Robert Stroud in his hospital cell.

Robert Miller sat on a cot in a tiny Alcatraz cell. It was 1935, and he was wearing a drab prison inmate's uniform stamped with the number 300. He had come a long way from his upper-middle-class childhood home in what is now the Czech Republic.

Before he was locked up on Alcatraz, this man had wined and dined amongst the glamour and glitter of the wealthiest people in the world.

We don't like criminals. Criminals hurt people. That's why we put them in prison!

But there's one type of criminal whom we sometimes ... sort of ... admire. People like Count Lustig. He was a cheat, a charlatan, an imposter, a counterfeiter, and a scoundrel. In spite of that, people liked him. (He even pulled a scam on Al Capone!) He was the King of the Con Men.

A good con man is an actor, someone who tricks and cheats people who are greedy and dishonest.

In the 1920s, Robert Miller spent the last of his money on flashy clothes and a first-class ticket on a trans-Atlantic ocean liner. That would give him plenty of time to schmooze with the richest people of the day as they lounged on board and looked for ways to entertain themselves.

He introduced himself as Count Victor Lustig. A good listener, he also seemed to be humble despite being "royalty." He made other people feel fascinating and important. He drew them in. Eventually, he chose someone he thought might be at least a little bit dishonest, and pretended to take that person into his confidence.

He would admit that he owned a money-making box.

Would that person be shocked that Count Lustig was a counterfeiter, and go to the police? No. Lustig knew how to choose well. His new friend would want to see the box at work.

It was amazing! First, he inserted a $100 bill. He'd wait a day while some "chemicals" did their work (this time lag was important). Then he'd turn a roller and TWO $100 bills would come out!

His new friend would want a money-making box, too. Well, Count Lustig would say, it's very valuable to me. I might sell it . . . but only because you're such a good friend.

Count Lustig did this trick time and time again. His "good friends" gave him $10,000, $20,000, and once, $46,000! Each time, Lustig would reluctantly part with his precious box.

How did the box work? It was just a plain wooden box salted with a few real $100 bills. While the ship was at sea, the machine would roll out $100 bills like clockwork. But once the ship landed and everyone parted ways, the box would stop working. At some point, the buyer would realize that he (or she) had been tricked.

Buyers couldn't go to the police and complain that someone had sold them a fake counterfeiting machine! And they'd feel far too foolish to tell their friends.

As good as that con was, Count Lustig had much, much bigger plans. He went to Paris.

It's hard to imagine Paris without the Eiffel Tower, but in the 1920s, the city was thinking of scrapping it. It had been built to be only a temporary part of the 1889 World's Fair, and it was rusting. Still, the people of Paris didn't want it torn down.

Lustig gathered a group of scrap dealers. It was true, he told them. The tower was coming down. He told them that he worked for the city, and that his assignment was to choose which scrap-metal company got the job. That company would pay $50,000, and then when it tore down the tower, it could sell all that metal. The company who got the job would make a fortune. They had to keep this information to themselves, however.

A common con man might have left it at that. But Lustig always targeted the man he thought was the greediest and most dishonest. He told one man that he'd make sure he got the contract. All he had to do was pay an extra $20,000 as a bribe. The man paid Lustig $70,000. Then Lustig disappeared.

What really makes Lustig the King of the Con Men was that he returned to Paris and pulled off this scam again!

Eventually, Lustig turned to real money counterfeiting, and was caught in New York and sent to jail, where he was locked up in a cell on the third floor. One day, the jailer noticed that he was gone! Lustig had torn up his bed sheets, tied them together into a rope, then used the rope to lower himself down the wall. As he dangled his way to the ground, he stopped at each window and pretended he was a window-washer. Dozens of passersby saw him. No one paid attention to the window-washer wearing prison clothes.

Eventually, Lustig was picked up, and his exciting years of exotic scams came crashing down on him. He was sentenced to twenty years and sent away to Alcatraz, where he went back to being plain Robert Miller, prisoner A7-300. After about a dozen years at Alcatraz, he came down with pneumonia and died.

The death certificate of the man who had sold the Eiffel Tower—twice—listed his occupation as "apprentice salesman."

the INMATE who CAME BACK from the DEAD

It doesn't seem possible for a man to come back from the dead. And yet that's just what Floyd Hamilton (AZ-523) did!

When Floyd went to Alcatraz with a thirty-year sentence hanging over his head, he had a wife and an eight-year-old daughter, Betty Joyce. His wife divorced him, and children couldn't visit their fathers at Alcatraz.

Do you know which prisoners are the most dangerous? The ones with nothing to lose. Floyd's family was gone. He had nothing to lose. So when an opportunity to take part in an escape came up, Floyd jumped at it.

World War II was being fought and Floyd was working with just a few men at the north end of the island, next to a building where prisoners were laundering military uniforms. The building Floyd was working in was old, and it was near a cliff that went straight into the water. Floyd and his three cronies came up with an elaborate escape plan.

The first part involved the bars. The men cut through some of the bars, then puttied and painted them so they looked solid and stayed in place.

The next thing they needed was clothes to replace their prison uniforms. Floyd and the men smuggled four military uniforms out of the laundry and put them in large, empty paint cans. Those cans would help them in two ways. First, the men planned to use the cans as flotation devices. Second, when they got to shore, they would have dry military uniforms to wear. Have you ever heard the term, "hiding in plain sight"? That's what they would do. San Francisco was filled with thousands of soldiers. They would just blend in.

The day came, and they put their plan into effect. They beat and then tied up their guards. But when they tried to go out the window, they realized they had made a terrible mistake. The opening they cut wasn't big enough to get the cans through. They had to leave them (and the uniforms they contained) behind. They went out the window anyway, and scrambled down the cliff to the bay.

They were discovered missing almost immediately. Boats full of guards with rifles circled the island. A guard shot one inmate in the head, and he slipped beneath the waves, dead. Guards fished two more out of the water. Then, something confusing happened. One of the guards swore he had shot Floyd Hamilton, and that Floyd had also gone beneath the waves. After a while, the search for Floyd was called off.

Daily News

DEAD!

The prison announced to the newspapers that the famous outlaw, Floyd Hamilton, was dead. His picture was in newspapers all over the United States.

So, where was Floyd? There were caves in the cliffs of Alcatraz, and those caves were stuffed with trash washed in by the currents. Floyd managed to wiggle his way into that trash to hide.

He stayed in the cave for three days and nights. The water was too salty to drink. He had no food. It was cold. He must have shivered the whole time. Crabs bit his toes. Finally, Floyd realized he'd never be able to swim to the city. If he didn't do something, he would soon die. But what could he do?

Floyd climbed back up the cliff and broke into Alcatraz. A guard walked into a room and found Floyd asleep against a radiator. Floyd Hamilton was back from the dead.

Unfortunately, Floyd really didn't learn anything from his

escape. He tried to escape several times more. But one day, Floyd's life changed. His daughter, Betty Joyce—by then, grown, married, and with children of her own—wrote to him. Floyd realized that the best way to get out of prison so he could spend time with Betty Joyce and his grandchildren was to stop trying to escape and to follow every rule. If you follow every rule in prison, you can often get out of prison early.

His good behavior paid off. But just before he got out of prison, something very sad happened. Betty Joyce died. However, his ex-wife Mildred was waiting for him. They remarried. Though Floyd did not raise his daughter, he did raise his grandson and granddaughter.

Floyd loved giving talks to people. He tried to convince them to live good lives and do good deeds. In one of his talks, he said,

"Lucky for me, Alcatraz became my birthplace and not my grave."

This was in interesting comment for a man who came back from the dead!

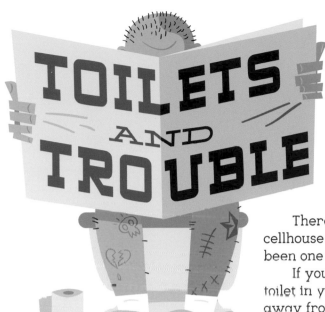

TOILETS AND TROUBLE

At one time, there were more than 600 toilets on the little 22-acre island of Alcatraz.

There were 600 in the cellhouse alone; it must have been one stinky place!

If you were an inmate, the toilet in your cell was inches away from your bed. Sweet dreams! Most of the cells had cells facing them. When you used the toilet, you had no privacy. A dozen inmates and any number of guards could watch you.

Oddly, when the prison was first built, toilets were a luxury. In 1912, many Americans didn't have toilets inside their houses. They had to go outside to a wooden outhouse with bugs and spiders. Some didn't have sinks with running water—they used basins they filled from a bucket of water that had been hand pumped from a well outside. So when the prison first opened, each prisoner's cell was rather grand, with its very own sink and toilet.

Prisoners made small breaks in the porcelain at the base of the toilet to hide things such as notes or shivs. They patched the hole with wet toilet paper—kind of like papier-mâché.

When the prison was in operation, all the raw sewage from the island went straight into the bay. People were disgusted with this and wanted it to stop.

Some say Alcatraz closed in 1963 because of the two embarrassing 1962 escape attempts. But perhaps sewage also played a part.

STRANGE BUT TRUE

Prisoners who were locked up alone in the dark cells in solitary confinement found a way to talk to other inmates. If an inmate in the D Block scooped all the water out the toilet, he could talk to an inmate in a dark cell using the sewage pipe as a telephone line!

HELLOOO

DUMMY HEAD ESCAPE !

Early on the morning of June 12, 1962, one of the Alcatraz officers was angry. Three lazy inmates wouldn't get up after the morning whistle had blown—they just lay in their beds with their eyes closed, heads nestled in their pillows.

"I'll get them up!" another officer called, and slapped one of the pillows to waken the man.

The inmate's head fell off and clattered to the floor!

It wasn't a real head, of course. It was made of cloth, wire, soap, and paper. But the inmate's cell and two others were empty! The escape sirens began to wail.

Months earlier, an inmate named Alan West (AZ-1335) was assigned a new job at the prison: maintenance. He was to paint and fix things that were broken. This gave him access to lots of tools and materials and, best of all, allowed him to travel all over the prison. In the area above the B Block utility corridor, he made an important discovery. There was a vent in the ceiling, a vent that led onto the roof. It was a way off the Rock!

There were lots of bars in the vent that would have to be cut and then bent back. It would take a long time. However, time is something inmates have a lot of.

Soon, he pulled together a team of men for an escape attempt. Over the course of several weeks, inmates Frank Morris (AZ-1441) and two brothers, Clarence and John Anglin (AZ-1485 and AZ-1476), cut into the old cement walls of their B Block cells around the vent grates, making openings big enough for them to get through and into the utility corridor. They disguised the cuts with sections of fake walls that could be removed whenever they wanted.

After the holes were big enough, every night they would remove the grates, climb out of their cells and up the pipes to the top of B Block, and cut and bend the bars inside the vent.

But it wasn't to be quite that easy.

Several times each night, guards walked down the aisles. They made a count of inmates sleeping in their cells. If anyone was missing, it would be discovered right away.

The men knew that it was rather dark in the cellhouse at night, and what the guards were counting was the sleeping heads on the pillows. So they came up with an idea.

Using many types of materials, they made "dummy heads," which they planned to leave on their pillows. The heads were even covered with real hair from the barbershop!

Alan West didn't work above B Block at night, and he took his time cutting through the cement at the back of his cell. But he did work up there almost every day and was able to smuggle in many materials. The men made rafts and life vests out of raincoats, and paddles out of wood.

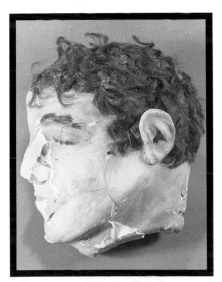

John Anglin dummy head.

On the night of June 11, 1962, Morris and the Anglin brothers finally bent the last bar. They would soon be free! One of the men went to the back of Alan West's cell to tell him the time had come.

The thing was, Alan West had not finished cutting through the wall. He wasn't going anywhere.

The men left a life vest in the corridor behind his cell, then dragged the raft, the other vests, and a concertina (similar to an accordion) up through the vent with them.

Carrying all these things, they ran the length of the cellhouse, lowered themselves down a pipe to the ground far below, climbed over some barbed-wire fences, and made their way to the water's edge.

Why did they bring the concertina? Did they want music that badly? No! They were going to use it as a bellows to inflate the raft.

Then they disappeared into the cold and unforgiving bay, never to be heard from again.

Did the flimsy raft sink, plunging them into the waves and death by drowning? Did they get swept out through the Golden Gate to the Pacific Ocean, only to be ravaged by sharks? Was there a boat to pick them up, manned by someone who would keep their secret for more than fifty years? We will probably never know.

And what about Alan West? Why did he stay behind?

Perhaps he meant to. There is a saying, "Better the devil you know than the devil you don't." What this means is that people prefer things that are familiar, even if those things are bad or uncomfortable. As bad as prison was, Alan West understood prison, and was comfortable there. Most likely, he chose prison over the unknown of the inky black water of San Francisco Bay.

West was moved from one prison to the next. Once he was

released, he only lasted a year before he committed more crimes and was returned. Then he murdered another inmate.

His was not a happy life, but one thing made him happy. For the rest of his short life, he had bragging rights to perhaps the best-known prison escape in the United States.

Until he died at the young age of 49, West would tell the story to anyone who would listen.

Perhaps, after all, that was enough for the sad, small life of Alan West.

PROTEST SITE
ALCATRAZ

Alcatraz Is INDIAN LAND

By 1969, the prison had been closed for six years. There were only two people living on Alcatraz. They were caretakers of a peaceful and empty island.

Then one day, a large boat drew close to the island. Suddenly, dozens of people, mostly young men, threw themselves off the boat and into the cold water. They swam to the island and pulled themselves onto the rocks.

They were American Indians from many different tribes.

They announced to the caretaker, "This island is now Indian land!"

Did American Indians originally live on Alcatraz Island hundreds of years ago? The answer is simple: no. People need water to live, and there is no fresh water source on Alcatraz

Island. The bay water is far too salty to drink; people can die within a few days of drinking only bay water. The island had no plants, no trees to provide shade, no food (except sea birds and their eggs) to eat. It would be an entirely miserable island to try to live on.

For thousands of years, all across the North American continent, native people lived on whatever land was best for them—land that had food and water and other things they needed to live a good life. Then, beginning in the 1500s, people came from other continents and wanted that land, so the American Indians had to either move or fight. Three hundred years later, the fighting was over, and the American government relocated the defeated tribes onto lands that were of little value—land that no one wanted. Eventually, those lands became home.

In 1969, native people across the United States had a lot to be angry and sad about. Many of them were again being forced to move away from their homes.

Fifteen years before, the American government began to shut down reservations across the United States. All the people who lived there were given bus tickets to cities. By 1969, more than one hundred reservations had been eliminated and their people had been scattered around the country.

If the groups didn't live together, their people would eventually lose their languages, their ceremonies, their music, their religions, their dances and stories. Their traditions might be lost forever.

Finally, they had had enough, and decided to protest. They needed a way to get their story into the newspapers so everyone would know what was happening to them. Many of them had been sent to live in cities in the San Francisco Bay Area, and could see Alcatraz and its many empty buildings. This gave them an idea.

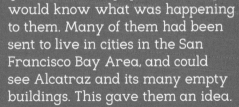

They knew that if they landed on Alcatraz Island and tried to live there—if they occupied it—their plight would become worldwide news.

They were right. Newspapers and TV shows all over the world announced the occupation. What the occupiers were doing was illegal, the same way that Rosa Parks was breaking the law when she refused to give up her bus seat to a white man. She was willing to break the law and go to jail for her beliefs. It was the same with the protestors.

Richard Nixon was president at that time. He knew that what the occupiers were doing was against the law, but he told the US Marshals to stay off the island, and not to arrest them. After all, he thought, how long could they stay on an island without food, water, or jobs? Soon, they would have to leave on their own, and that way, no one would get hurt.

Nixon forgot one thing, however: there are millions of people in the San Francisco Bay Area and many were on the protestors' side, and were willing to send them the things they needed.

The occupiers had been on the island for three months when a tragedy happened.

A thirteen-year-old girl named Yvonne Oakes, the stepdaughter of the occupiers' spokesman, fell to her death in one of the apartment buildings.

Everyone was heartbroken. Many—including Yvonne's mother and stepfather—left the island. They felt the price they had paid for the protest had been too high. Others stayed and continued the protest.

As the months went by, things became more and more confused, complicated, and chaotic. Other people came to the island, and there were disagreements about what they should be doing. Some brought weapons, and used them!

Then one night, about a year after Yvonne's death, fires erupted.

An arsonist set fire to five historic buildings. Three of them burnt to the ground. Two of them were left as shells.

The occupiers never claimed they set the fires (some said government undercover agents were responsible). But the public felt angry about the historic buildings being burned. They began to distrust the protest and its leaders. They stopped sending food, water, and money. Eventually, hardships drove most of the occupiers off the island. The few who remained were removed by US Marshals in June 1971. (No one was prosecuted.)

The story didn't end the way those who occupied the island wanted it to. Alcatraz did not become Indian land. But important things happened, anyway. Congress reversed some of the laws and stopped closing reservations, and some of the land that had been taken was returned to the tribes.

Today, Alcatraz Island is an important symbol for all of the country's native people. It marked the beginning of the American Indian Movement, a time during which people began to relearn and save their traditions in earnest.

Three times a year, thousands of American Indians from all over the country gather on the Rock for sunrise ceremonies. Anyone can attend, and watch the dancing, singing, and speeches.

Because of Alcatraz Island, American Indian traditions were saved!

The occupiers put up this tipi, symbolic of traditional American Indian life, as a sign that they had taken back the island.

MAKING A STATEMENT

During the federal prison years, a simple, white "United States Penitentiary" sign announced the rules in huge letters to boaters, prison visitors, and residents alike. When the prison closed, the sign was replaced with one announcing that the island was "United States Property."

Then, when the occupiers showed up in 1969, they modified the sign to read "United Indian Property." As part of their protest, they established a kind of "immigration station" in the dock area. During the early days of the occupation, people coming onto the island had to prove that they were Indians in order to stay overnight.

A non-Indian caretaker who was there before the Indians arrived also lived on the island. For a while, he kept a running count of people who came and went, listing them in one of two categories: Indians or Hippies!

When Alcatraz came under the care of the National Park Service, the old "United States Penitentiary" sign was put up again, and the occupiers' notice was also left in place. It makes for a confusing sight. The red painted "AN" (from the word INDI-AN) is almost all that can be seen on the wall behind it.

Federal Prison Era
1934 - 1963

Note: The acreage on the sign is wrong; the island is actually 22 acres.

Indian Occupation
1969 - 1971

National Park Service
1972 - Present Day

The dock sign isn't the only one the occupiers changed. Over the doorway to the administration wing is an emblem that some call the Alcatraz Eagle, or the Eagle Crest: roughly six feet wide and three feet tall, it tells a story of America in its symbols, especially the eagle and the shield with its thirteen stars and thirteen stripes.

In the beginning, the occupiers hung a handmade sign around the eagle's neck. Later, that sign was taken down and a secret message was painted into the shield itself. That message can still be seen today.

Thousands of people look up at that crest every day, but almost no one notices the secret message left by the Indians.

The occupiers painted their message everywhere, including on the island's water tower.

ADMINISTRATION BUILDING

Entrance to the prison's Administration wing. Do you see the secret message hidden in the shield the eagle's perching on?

CELLHOUSE

NATIONAL PARK
ALCATRAZ

WHAT IF YOU HAD THE KEYS TO ALCATRAZ?

What would you do if you had the keys to Alcatraz? The island is now yours—would you leave it as it is, a national park site visited by more than a million people every year? Would you turn it into an expensive resort catering to the richest of the rich? Would you make it a symbol—perhaps a beacon of hope?

This is what the government had to decide in 1963, when the prison was closed and the inmates were sent to other prisons. For years, the only people on the island were its caretakers. During this time, many people and groups debated what to do with these 22 acres of rock just over a mile from the beautiful city of San Francisco.

Imaginations went wild. Almost no one thought it would be a good idea to preserve the prison. How morbid! Why celebrate something so dark and sinister?

Ideas were collected by the San Francisco Public Library. Among them were:

1 Install a nuclear-powered water jet that would shoot water hundreds of feet into the air like a geyser, then fall back on the prison, gradually eroding it into the bay.

2 Install a giant statue of St. Francis, patron saint of San Francisco.

3 Turn the buildings into giant planters full of vibrant flowers to be enjoyed by all the people surrounding the bay.

4 Hollow out the interior to make a bay within the bay.

5 Install a West Coast version of the Statue of Liberty.

6 Create a United Nations Peace Monument.

7 Mount giant cannons that could shoot hundreds of water missiles into forest fires across California.

Finally, after all the ideas had been debated, the federal government decided to sell the island to the City of San Francisco, but the city had to figure out where to get the money to buy it. Oddly, to buy it, they decided to sell it!

They almost sold the island to a man from Texas named Lamar Hunt. His plan was to use part of the island for a space monument, and convert another part into an 1890s-themed shopping mall.

For nineteen months, plans were on hold while the Indians of All Tribes occupied the island. By the time they left, a new idea began to grow.

Why not make it a national park site? Why not tear down the buildings and turn the island into something more natural, with plants and paths?

In 1972, Congress created Golden Gate National Recreation Area and included Alcatraz in it; the island was to be managed by the National Park Service. The NPS decided to offer a few tours of the prison buildings while they were still standing, but expected that people would eventually lose interest. Imagine everyone's surprise when these tours became so popular that they never stopped. Today, 5,000 people a day tour the prison.

What do the keys to Alcatraz really open? Perhaps it's the door to our imaginations, where our fears and our hopes live.

A futuristic view of Alcatraz, c. 1980.

HOLLYWOOD
dresses up
ALCATRAZ

Is everything on Alcatraz Island today "real?" Or has it been dressed up? When you file by the famous escape cells of 1962, are you seeing the real beds and fifty-year-old holes in the wall left by the escaped prisoners? Or did the National Park Service build replicas?

Some of the cells at Alcatraz are full of items that make the cell look like it would have when the prisoners were there. The NPS has "dressed" those cells. But those items can be removed in minutes. The NPS rarely changes things in a permanent way, such as painting or cutting holes.

While most things on Alcatraz Island today are real, some have been changed in the past. And almost always, the answer to "Who changed things?" is "Hollywood."

Today, the NPS is very strict about what moviemakers can do to the island. But years ago, the NPS might have been a bit star-struck. They shut down the island so movies could be filmed. They also allowed movie people to paint things and build things.

Still, some of those changes have ended up being helpful to visitors. For instance, the control room for the prison was mostly dismantled and destroyed when the prison closed down. Today— thanks to a 1987 movie, Six Against the Rock—the control room looks the way it would have in 1940s. The control room was rebuilt as a movie set, then left in place.

What is real today, and what are Hollywood props?

REAL OR PROPS?

① **THE 1962 MORRIS/ANGLIN ESCAPE DUMMY HEADS**

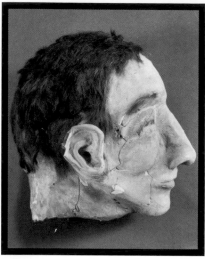

Frank Morris dummy head.

PROPS

The real dummy heads are safely stored in the archives located in San Francisco. These were made for the TV show *America's Most Wanted*.

② **HOLES IN THE BACK OF THE 1962 MORRIS/ANGLIN CELLS**

REAL

But when Hollywood was making the movie *Escape from Alcatraz* in the 1970s, it cut holes in the backs of other cells that were easier to film. The holes were later patched up. This would probably not be allowed today.

Senior officer Waldron in Frank Morris's cell, June 1962.

③ **THE VISITATION ROOM**

REAL

But stripped down. In 1963, the visitors' side of the room was carpeted and paneled, and looked inviting. When the movie *Murder in the First* was filmed here, all the niceties were removed so it would look more like it did back in the 1930s: cold and forbidding.

4 "DOCK," "GLOVE," AND "BRUSH" LINES ON THE RECREATION YARD CONCRETE

PROPS The badly faded original lines were repainted with NPS approval for the movie *Murder in the First.* The lines showed prisoners where to line up before being led to their workstations. Today, even these props have almost completely disappeared under the footsteps of millions of visitors

5 POOL TABLE IN THE GUARDS' BREAKROOM

REAL

When the prison closed, the pool table was taken off the island and eventually ended up in a San Francisco bar. It was used there for almost fifty years; then the bar had the pool table renovated and returned it to Alcatraz Island.

Sometimes it's impossible to tell real from props. But that's part of the fun of Hollywood!

WATER, WATER EVERYWHERE

Each year, more than 4,000 athletes successfully swim from Alcatraz to the San Francisco shoreline.

How do they do it? Why couldn't the inmates?

Swimmers today train for long hours. They're in excellent shape. Alcatraz inmates spent long hours in cramped cells or at their workstations. They could join a prison baseball team, but there was never an Alcatraz swim team!

Most swimmers today wear wetsuits to protect themselves from the cold water. Still, several hundred swimmers also cross the bay without wetsuits. With daily training in the cold water, it can be done. The bay is about 50 degrees year-round. That's not icy, but it's much colder than your body's 98-degree temperature.

Most importantly, they know the timing of the bay's strong currents. The San Francisco Bay runs like a reversible river, changing directions four times a day at different times each day. No one—not even Olympic swimmers—can swim from the island to the city shoreline when the tides are running. They must swim in between currents, during a very short window of time called "slack tide."

Alcatraz inmates didn't understand the currents, and even if they did, they didn't have tide tables to look at. They also couldn't choose an exact time to escape and go into the water. That made the swim almost impossible.

Athletes have boats following them, keeping them safe.

These boats keep them on course and help them if they get too tired. Alcatraz inmates were followed by boats full of guards firing bullets at them!

Some very young swimmers have been successful in crossing the bay. In 2007, seven-year-old Braxton Bilbrey from Glendale, Arizona, completed the swim in 47 minutes to raise money for drowning-prevention efforts. In 2009, eight-year-old twin sisters Sarah and Hannah Parson made the swim. Older swimmers Gary Emich and Steve Hurwitz have each made the swim more than a thousand times!

STRANGE
BUT TRUE

A four-year-old Golden Retriever named Jake dog-paddled his way from Alcatraz to the San Francisco shore, finishing in 42 minutes. He came in 72nd out of 500 swimmers. Jake's owner said that when the dog was asked what the water was like, he answered, "Ruff!"

BURIED TREASURE

Could there really be buried treasure on Alcatraz Island?

Yes! Alcatraz Island is still giving up its secrets.

In 2006, staff members on the island pulled a huge shelving unit away from a wall so they could paint it, and a long, heavy shiv clattered to the floor. A shiv is a nasty, prisoner-made knife. This was the type of shiv that could kill a man or maim him badly.

Had the shiv been used? The shelving unit was in the clothing issue room next to the showers. It's quite possible that one inmate had knifed another in the shower, passed the shiv through the

wire fence into the clothing issue room, and the worker there had hidden it, only for it to be discovered fifty years later. Or was it a hoax? When the movie *Escape from Alcatraz* was being filmed, the props department was located in the clothing-issue area. Did a props person make the shiv and hide it, hoping that it might tumble out, just as it did, decades in the future, and fool everyone?

In 2010, while crews were fixing the roof of the morgue, they discovered a piece of cloth stuck in some machinery. What was interesting about the cloth was that it came from an inmate's shirt, with the inmate's number sewn on. Did an inmate leave it there so he'd be remembered? We'll probably never know, but most likely, the inmate had been released from the prison and his shirt was simply torn up to make rags.

In 2014, a little girl with sharp eyes noticed a ball in a pile of weeds and leaves just on the other side of a fence. She did the right thing and told a ranger. The ball was down the hill from an area that used to be a playground for the guards' families. Most likely, a child was sorry when that toy was lost more fifty years ago!

Might there be other items hidden on Alcatraz? It seems likely. There could be more shivs or notes or other things that we can't even imagine.

Who knows what might be found, and who might find it? If you're ever on Alcatraz Island, it could even be you!

STRANGE
BUT TRUE

Everything on Alcatraz is protected; it's against the rules to remove anything from the island. Over the years, rocks taken illegally have been mailed back, along with letters describing years of bad luck. To lift the jinx, the letter-writers often ask Alcatraz rangers to return the bits of stone to the exact spot from which they were stolen.

COWBIRDS

THUGS OF THE BIRD WORLD

There's more to Alcatraz than prison cells. Lush gardens and songbirds soften the Rock. Alcatraz is also an important nesting site for many seabirds. But it's fitting that it's sometimes the home of cowbirds, the "thugs of the bird world."

Like all birds, cowbirds lay eggs. Just not in their own nests. They lay their eggs in other birds' nests. Such a hassle to build a nest and sit on your own eggs! Too much trouble to protect and feed hungry babies! Such a nuisance to help your kids learn to fly and hunt for food on their own!

Poor little warblers are the usual birds the cowbirds choose to adopt their eggs. The warblers have to do more than double duty to raise their own offspring and the much, much larger cowbird babies.

But it gets better. Or worse. Scientists decided to see what would happen if they removed cowbird eggs from the warbler nests. They thought that cowbirds laid their eggs then flew away. But they were wrong.

The cowbirds might not be raising their own young, but they made darn sure another bird was.

Like gangsters, the cowbirds resorted to violence, smashing the warblers' eggs when their own eggs were removed.

What's a warbler to do? Just take care of anything and everything in your nest. Feed that great big cowbird mouth. Work, work, work, 24/7.

And never, ever cross a cowbird!

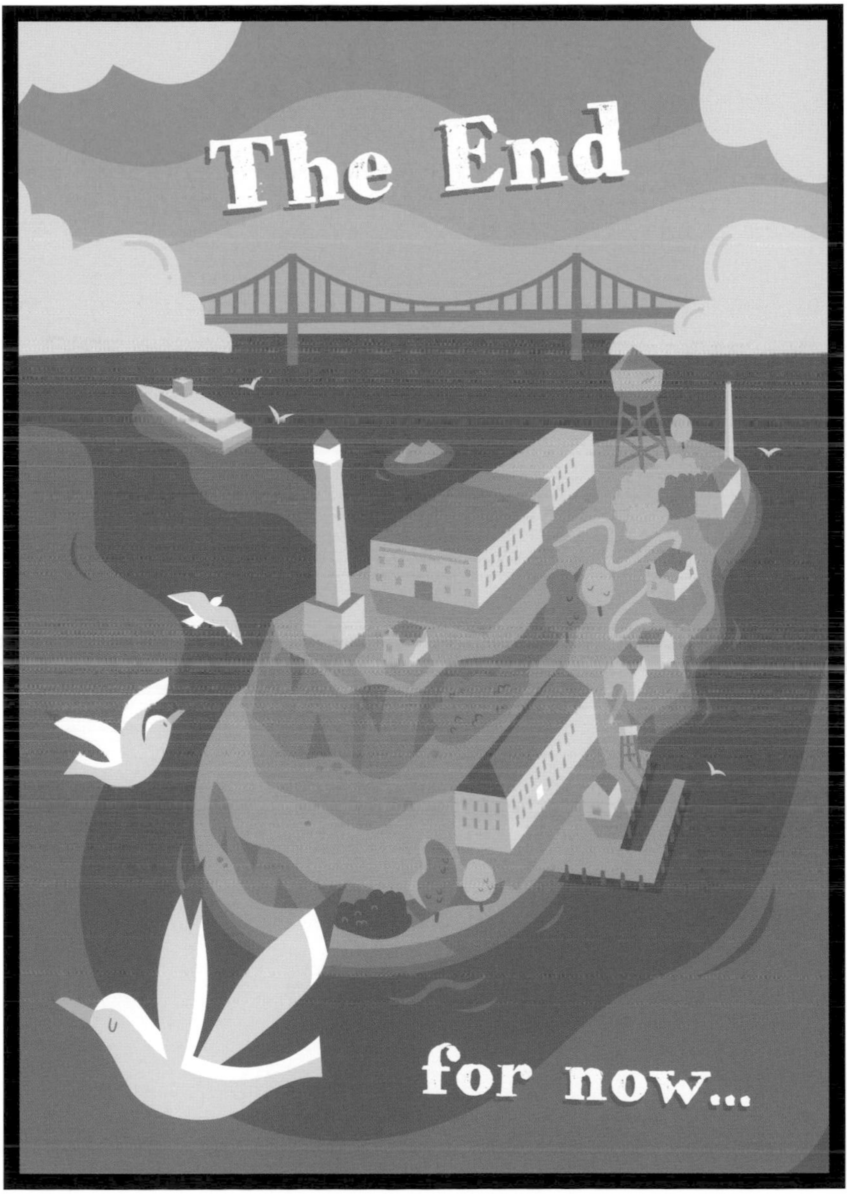
The End
for now...

ACKNOWLEDGMENTS

FROM THE AUTHOR

Grateful thanks to my fellow interpreters on the Alcatraz Night Tour, and to Jolene Babyak, Michael Esslinger, Eric Knackmuhs, John Moran, John Cantwell, Bennie Batom, Lori Brosnan, Nicki Phelps, and Teresa Williams for your support and for sharing your stories with me.

This book was whipped into shape by my editor/wizard Susan Tasaki; my thanks.

Three cheers for the National Park Service!

And my never-ending gratitude to my sister Kathleen, who began writing down my stories when I was three and started me on my writer's path.

FROM THE PUBLISHER

We are fortunate to work with wonderful National Park Service colleagues who support, collaborate, challenge, and guide us in creating publications that help visitors understand and appreciate Alcatraz Island's unique history and features. Supervisor of Interpretation Marcus Koenen offered particular support (in this and many projects), which is instrumental to our success.

On the Parks Conservancy side, we would like to acknowledge the creative team: Charles House for his exceptional illustrations and design, and Vivian Young, who guided them; our editor, Susan Tasaki, whose judgment and know-how shaped and focused the book; and Sarah Lau Levitt, and Sandy Chu who skillfully managed its production.

For championing our publications to visitors, we also thank our entire Alcatraz retail team, led by Elizabeth Siahaan, Lala Macapagal, Colin Fairbairn, Lulu Sera, Maggie Rosario and Jillian Kelling. We thank the Parks Conservancy's Executive Vice President and Chief Operating Officer Nicolas Elsishans for encouraging us to explore new opportunities and realize our vision.

Finally, we thank author T. C. Bakker for having such a splendid idea.

AUTHOR

T. C. Bakker

has been a historic interpreter on Alcatraz
Island for 10 years.

ILLUSTRATOR

Charles House

is an illustrator and designer for the Golden
Gate National Parks Conservancy. He lives in
Oakland, California.